D0949430

Aggression
and
Altruism

Concern for the welfere of
others

152.43
K162

Aggression
and
Altruism

A PSYCHOLOGICAL ANALYSIS

Harry Kaufmann

Hunter College of the City University of New York

112156

LIBRARY ST. MARY'S COLLEGE

WITHDRAWN
ST. MARYS COLLEGE LIBRARY

HOLT, RINEHART AND WINSTON, INC.

New York   Chicago   San Francisco   Atlanta
Dallas   Montreal   Toronto   London   Sydney

Copyright © 1970 by Holt, Rinehart and Winston, Inc.
All rights reserved
Library of Congress Catalog Card Number: 78-97846
SBN: 03-078085-3
Printed in the United States of America
9 8 7 6 5 4 3 2 1

PREFACE

Man has long studied himself with great patience and wonderment, but also with a smattering of sensationalism. Quite often, he has been more interested in situations of conflict, of war, and of bloodshed than in familial bliss, in the joys of the exploration of nature, and in the delights of introspective contemplation. Even today, what sells a newspaper may be news of the tragedy of a family burnt in a house, of an automobile accident involving multiple deaths, or of the violent attack of a gang upon a helpless bystander. Violence, disaster, and death seem to be the daily source of diversion, even entertainment, for a very large number of individuals—not excluding adolescents and children. But it would be begging the question to ascribe this particular interest simply to a depravation of tastes, or more simply still to say: "Well, this is the way others might feel, but not, of course, you and I." We must, in other words, be concerned with *why* such a large majority of people do find this type of news or information interesting, even fascinating. However regrettable they might be, the sufferings of others form a substantial part of the average person's daily concerns.

Yet when "aggression" was proposed as the topic of this book, I alternately approached and withdrew from the task with a vague sense of discomfort. Somehow, I felt as if I were about to write the type of book which, under the guise of horrifying the reader by presenting him with an extensive catalogue of human depravity, in reality derived its appeal from his attraction to those very horrors.

Also, several important works had only recently examined aggression in animals and man far more completely than could be done in this modest-sized volume. But the deciding factor in the emergence of the present format was probably the observation that such terms as "aggression," "anxiety," and "frustration" have for the layman and even a number of experts, acquired meanings that go beyond attempts at rigorous definitions. They have become almost like things or entities presumed to have an existence of their own.

Also, it would appear that aggression is seen as a more "natural," more "basic" behavior than what might be considered its obverse, "altruism." Freud, for instance, would assign expression of aggression to the "id," but would presumably limit manifestations of love and justice to the "superego." Finally, it is perhaps as a consequence of the considerations mentioned above, as well as of the nature of the behaviors involved, that we can readily visualize too much aggression (for the viability of the group), but not too much altruism (although it is possible to conceive of such an extreme).

There have been, it is true, some statements to the effect that cooperation, altruism, and self-sacrifice are "more basic" to the "laws of life" than destructive behaviors. For instance, Montagu (1950) blames a misinterpretation of Darwin for giving the man in the street what he considers to be the mistaken idea that conflict is the law of life. The prejudices of a class, he suggests, were mistaken for the laws of nature. It was very convenient for those who were benefiting from the Industrial Revolution to justify exploitation of others on the grounds that life is a struggle for existence, and that the strong survive. These ideas, it would seem, can become a self-fulfilling prophecy, for Montagu asserts that they govern most behavior in the Western world today, and that they plunged us into a "sorry state of personal, interpersonal, and international conflict" (p. 21). Actually, "cooperative behavior is at least as prominent a form of interaction between animals under natural conditions as is conflict or competition" (p. 22). Haldane (1935) is quoted by Montagu as saying that in the struggle for existence, "altruistic behavior is a kind of Darwinian fitness." Or, as Kropotkin wrote in 1902, mutual aid increases survival values for all forms of life. But these authors were, in fact, making their point in rebuttal to the advocates of a basic destructive urge.

To write a separate study of a topic such as aggression is essentially equivalent to considering aggression as qualitatively different from other psychological areas of inquiry. I never was quite sure that this presumed hierarchy of processes is justified, and this doubt continued to beset me for the several years during which I have occupied myself with matters pertaining to what popularly would be called aggressive behavior.

But if it is really doubtful that there exists, or that it makes sense to speak of, "aggression" as behavior in a class by itself, then there is no good reason for studying specifically that slice of behavior. Granted, we might point out that people have maimed and killed each other, under a variety of pretexts, since the beginning of recorded history, and unless the race is to destroy itself, we had better find out why, and whether anything can be done about it. But suppose we rephrase the problem to read as follows: How can we best approach the study of those forms of social interaction which are somehow related to the commission of injurious acts? We begin then, with the basic assumption that "aggression is most profitably viewed as *one* form of social behavior—which above all cannot be examined in a vacuum, apart from all other forms of human interaction.

From this assumption it would then follow that we might also look at the obverse class; that is, those behaviors that consist of one human being furthering the well-being of another for personal reasons such as gratitude, conscience, self-gain, or perhaps because this simply seems to be the appropriate behavior for a given situation.

Such an approach has its difficulties; for, as we shall see, various mysterious and deep-lying factors can be adduced to account for man's inhumanity to man, and for nature's cruelty in general. Also, as we shall see, definitions of "aggression" tend to differ. We therefore cannot even start our examinations without clarifying the meanings of our terms.

To sum up, then, it is our purpose to examine social interactions, with particular emphasis on those interactions that are aimed at, or result in damage or injury to at least one of the participants or, conversely, in the well-being, the benefit, or the advantage to at least one of the participants. In doing so, we shall try to make no a priori assumptions as to the basic nature of destructive—or, for that matter—beneficial tendencies.

Harry Kaufmann

New York, N.Y.
November 1969

CONTENTS

ix

I

A Definition of "Aggression" and Aggression-related Terms

It is proposed that even experts disagree on a definition of the term "aggression." Classifying a behavior as "aggressive" implies a meaning that goes beyond the observed act, and can be defined as "purpose," "intent," or, preferably, "expectation." A working definition of the term, therefore, excludes nonhuman behavior, fantasy, and wholly accidential events. Aggression, hostility and anger are distinct, but their interrelationships can be usefully studied.

THE TERM "AGGRESSION," though it seems at first sight to have a very clear meaning, is really open to a number of different interpretations. We can perhaps agree that at a very low level of definition "aggression" is in some way related to attack or injury, usually where more than one participant is involved (although even here we run into a snag, because suicide has quite frequently, and with considerable logical justification, been called an aggressive act).

"Aggression," in other words, has been a global term, much like "anxiety" or "frustration," and as such has meant many different things to many people.

Our definitional problems therefore will be problems of exclusion as well as of inclusion. We shall look at a large class of behavior that we shall not wish to call "aggression," even though it does meet the very gross criterion stated above. Conversely, we shall also wish to include a number of rather subtle phenomena where aggression, again according to our low-level definition, is not at all obvious, but which, as I shall attempt to show, should be considered as aggressive behavior, if a theoretical formulation is to have any consistency.

All too often, not only laymen but psychologists, psychiatrists, and social scientists have used the term as if it were unequivocal in its meaning for all concerned. Even where attempts at definition have been made, they have suffered from insufficient or excessive scope, and neither their vagueness nor their occasional pseudoprecision has helped much toward establishing a theoretical framework capable of unambiguous empirical verification.

It might be objected at this point that, after all, most people manage to understand one another quite well when they speak of aggression, and that the issues examined in this chapter are therefore largely trivial. But this agreement is present only as long as the discourse remains vague, or where the discussion revolves around what might be called the "common core" of definitions.

Presumably, laymen and theoreticians alike would concur in defining as aggression an attack of A upon B, committed with every indication of anger, and followed by A's rejoicing at B's injury. The problem arises when other, less obvious situations are considered.

It might, therefore, be of value to consider, on the one hand, definitions offered by a dictionary and by some experts of human behavior, and on the other, a number of situations dealing with injury or attack. We might then examine the situations with two questions in mind: (1) Do they fit into traditional definitions of aggression? and (2) Is the clarity of discourse best served either by including or by excluding them in a new definition which we might wish to propose? *The Oxford Universal Dictionary* (1955) has this to say:

> Aggression: **1.** An unprovoked attack; the
> first attack in a quarrel; an assault. **2.** The
> practice of making such attacks.

This definition is only minimally helpful. First of all, it does not tell us the meaning of "attack" or "assault." It says nothing about the target of the attack; it is not clear whether only physical acts are involved, though this seems to be implied. Finally, definition number one deals with a behavior, whereas the second definition describes a tendency or habit; in other words, a construct inferred from observations.

A traditional definition of "aggression" is that offered by Dollard, Miller, Doob, Mowrer, and Sears in their well-known work *Frustration and Aggression* (1939, p. 11): "A response having for its goal the injury of a living organism."

This definition has been criticized by Buss (1961, p. 3) because it seems to imply purpose or intent, and therefore would not qualify as "behavioral." He prefers the following: "a response that delivers noxious stimuli to another organism" This definition, as we can see, does away completely with any inference about the organism's intent and observes only its behavior. But this rigor immediately presents us with an insurmountable problem. Can we really judge an act as aggressive only in terms of its effects upon the recipient or victim? If we do so, we are first of all using a term laden with connotations in a new and easily misunderstood way. But what is more important, we are now not really assessing the behavior of the actor at all, but only its effects upon a target. These effects clearly may differ widely—a blow of the first may inflict serious injury, or it may be just laughed off. Does this alter the aggressive nature of the performance? It might therefore be useful to consider some instances of what has sometimes been called "aggression."

1. A spider eats a fly.
2. A lion slays his prey.
3. Two wolves fight for leadership of the pack.
4. A soldier shoots his enemy at the frontline.
5. The warden of a prison executes a convicted criminal.
6. The juvenile gang attacks members of another gang.
7. One man attacks another in a barroom.
8. Two men fight for a piece of bread.
9. A man "viciously" kicks a cat.
10. A woman, while cleaning a window, knocks over a flowerpot, which, in falling, injures a pedestrian.
11. A boy kicks a wastebasket.
12. An "angry" driver kicks his flat tire.
13. Mr. X, a notorious gossip, speaks disparagingly of many people of his acquaintance. (They may, or may not know about this.)
14. Mr. Y, known for his cutting tongue, yerbally tears his subordinate to shreds.
15. Mr. X, far more subtle in his ways, speaks with barely detectable, yet cutting, irony to those who fail to live up to his expectations.
16. A boy has a dream, in which violence is committed either by him or against him, or in which he witnesses violence among others.
17. An enraged boy tries with all his might to inflict injury on his antagonist, a bigger boy, but is not successful in doing so. His efforts simply amuse the other boy.
18. A man daydreams of harming his antagonist, but has no expectation or hope of doing so.
19. A man mentally "rehearses" a murder he is about to commit.

Some of these examples may seem trivial, but examining only a few of them should show that we are dealing with genuine problems of definition. For instance, Buss's definition applies to case 1. The case does not fit in too well with the definition that assumes an inner state such as "intent." But after all, the traditional frustration-aggression definition does not speak of "intent"; it speaks of a "goal," and we do, in fact, speak of goal-directed behavior in animals too, so that by both definitions we have considered, the spider eating a fly is an act of aggression. Instances 2 and 3 are quite similar. Case 4 is a little peculiar; the soldier who shoots his enemy in battle is supposedly acting under orders, and in fact quite often has no hatred for his victim. Can we call acts of "pure obedience" aggression? And, moreover, what de we do in the case of the soldier who does perhaps derive just a little thrill out of extinguishing the life of another? A quite similar argument arises in the case of the warden (5). Cases 6 ,7, 8, and 9, at first sight, appear readily classifiable as aggressive by the definitions we have considered heretofore. Case 10 should also not give us any trouble: Who would think of accusing the poor lady of aggressing against an unknown pedestrian? But a definition that excludes intent and looks purely at the response would have to classify this response as an aggressive one because undoubtedly it did deliver a noxious stimulus to the hapless passerby.

Cases 11 and 12 would not be classified as aggression either by Dollard and his collaborators or by Buss, for it makes no sense to argue that wastebaskets or flat tires experience noxious stimuli. On the other hand, many psychiatrists and clinical psychologists would perhaps be very firm in considering this as aggressive behavior. They might argue, for instance, that the boy and the man really wanted to kick somebody, perhaps even themselves, and simply displaced their response upon the inanimate object. So, even in these two seemingly quite unequivocal cases we should run into arguments over definition. Can the gossip who speaks ill of others be called "aggressive" (case 13)? Perhaps it is not always clear that we can speak of a "goal" of his behavior, because he may speak ill of others without having any expectation at all that this behavior will injure or hurt them, in which case the strictly behavioral definition of "delivering a noxious stimulus" would not apply. But we can again see quite readily how this person would be rated by others as being "aggressive" or "hostile" (a word we shall define later).

We have no difficulty accommodating cases 14 and 15, despite the popular proverb "sticks and stones can break my bones but words will never hurt me," and despite, also, much legislation that provides far greater protection against physical than verbal injury. We know enough now to agree that verbal attack can be just as destructive in its effect, and just as vicious in its intent, as physical attack. And, as in case 4, the way in which this verbal attack occurs need not always be immediately obvious to the unsophisticated. Again, it is quite possible that both the speaker's intention and the effects upon the listener can be viewed in terms of an aggressive situation, even when aggression is communicated in a very subtle verbal way. Case 16 constitutes an autistic act, a dream. Clearly, we cannot speak of "effects upon others" because no others are affected. Does it make sense to speak of a "goal" on the part of the boy who has the dream? In terms of Freud's wish fulfillment we could say that the boy was dreaming out something which in waking life he could not attain. But Freud later admitted that anxiety too could produce fantasy behavior. Quite conceivably, the violence that the boy dreams might not be wish fulfillment but rather "repetition compulsion." In either case, we have to differentiate between the goal of dreaming and the goal of an act committed or observed in the dream. Case 17 is an instance in which one can safely diagnose "intent," but a noxious stimulus simply is never delivered, or is never perceived as being "noxious" by the target. In terms of Buss's definition, this would not then be an aggressive act.

Case 18, of the man daydreaming of injuring an enemy, is pure intent, without any behavioral component. Whatever it denotes in our evaluation of the daydreamer, it surely is not aggressive behavior. Again the clinician would probably have little difficulty in considering this situation as "aggressive," but neither Dollard's nor Buss's definition regard it as such.

Finally, case 19 is not at all difficult to classify as being a "preliminary to aggression." But is it in itself aggression? Is the goal of the act of rehearsing a future murder an "injury"? Certainly, at least at this stage, no noxious stimulus is being delivered.

NONHUMAN BEHAVIOR

There seems to be very little purpose in considering as "aggression" the enormous amount of interspecific mayhem which occurs in the infra-human animal world. If we were to do this, it would soon become quite evident that the very continuation of life presupposes endless slaughter across the species. It would simply enlarge our category beyond all useful bounds if we were to consider the eating of a fly by a spider or the hunting of a deer by a lion as aggressive behavior. The present volume focuses upon human behavior exclusively. The reason for this restriction is a simple one: this is not a natural history of aggression, but rather an examination of man's behavior toward his fellowman. Lorenz (1963) has examined the cycle of life and (sometimes violently produced) death in nature. Scott (1958) studied within-species animal aggression in a controlled laboratory setting. These studies enormously enhance our knowledge of animal behavior, but inferences and parallels to human behavior can be very misleading. This is especially the case when superficial similarities in behavior between, say, man and fish are explained in terms of instinctual forces common to both species. In the next chapter I shall examine the usefulness of this position for our purposes.

Similarly, we do not wish to consider the calling of the butcher an "aggressive" one. The slaughter of cattle or fowl for the ordinary nutritive purposes of man cannot, I believe, usefully be called "aggression." (The marginal case of the "sadistic" butcher who subjects his animals to unnecessary suffering or "visualizes" other people in his victims, falls into a special category, as might our case 9, of a man kicking a cat.) In general, therefore, we shall limit our study to events in which all participants are human.

INTENTION VERSUS ACCIDENT

Our definition excludes from our study those acts which, according to all observable indications, occur without expectations that harm to another person might result. I realize, of course, that a strong psychoanalytical case could be made for subconscious wishes, such as might be present in the woman who, while cleaning a window knocks over a flowerpot and injures a passerby below—he may resemble her husband. Until evidence to that effect is adduced, however, the act will not be considered an aggressive act.

FANTASY VERSUS ACTUAL BEHAVIOR

Several psychological tests and various studies have viewed eruptions of emotion, fantasied behavior, or interpretations of ambiguous stimuli, and have attached what are allegedly measures of aggression to (mainly verbal) behaviors emitted by the subject under these circumstances. For instance, TAT cards can be scored for aggression. Adjective checklists have been used to infer aggressive tendencies or intent on the part of the subject, and finally, daydreaming or dreams have been used to make similar inferences. It is of course possible for a person to imagine himself committing an aggressive act previous to executing the act, or at least with some expectation of executing it at some time in the future. On the other hand, a person may interpret an ambiguous picture or story, complete a phrase or a sentence, check adjectives, or even fantasy or dream of violent or injurious situations without in any way planning or expecting to engage in aggressive behavior. For our purposes these statements, fantasies, or interpretations will not be called "aggression." There is no objection, of course, to seeking relationships between such behaviors and aggression, but we should again be dealing with too many intangibles if we were to consider all these phenomena as constituting aggression.

EFFECTIVENESS: INJURY AS AN INCIDENTAL RESULT OF AGGRESSION

Where an act is initiated with the expectation of injuring another person, but fails to be consummated because of the other's superior defenses, or because of intervention of other forces, we shall nevertheless consider it an "aggressive" act. This example corresponds to our case

17: the enraged boy who tries, unsuccessfully, to inflict injury upon his bigger antagonist. Even in everyday usage one would certainly wish to classify such an act as "aggressive," regardless of its outcome.

OBEDIENCE AND AGGRESSION

We run into further difficulty when we consider killing for a cause such as "one's country" or "one's faith." It would be easy to say that this behavior should not be considered as "aggression," because it is, after all, committed not for the individual's own benefit; indeed, sometimes it is engaged in only at considerable cost and hardship. But we do have expectation, and frequent success. We might be tempted to exempt from the category of aggression those acts that are committed under extreme duress or strain—where disobedience to orders, for example, would be severely punished, and even where deviation from extremely strong social norms would be an act of unusual individual courage. Again, it is easy to see that the issue is by no means simple. What would we say, for instance, about the individual who is indeed under extreme constraint to commit violence, murder, or torture, but who obeys these instructions with slighty excessive alacrity? Would we consider him "aggressive," or would we simply say that he has committed an injurious act under compulsion and duress? Would we say that his obedience is "excessive"? Would we want to compare his obedience in this situation to obedience in other nonharmful situations? Even without this additional assumption injury to the enemy is at least a subgoal, and has behavioral and expectation components. For our purposes, therefore, expectation is present, and resulting behaviors would have to be considered "aggressive."

"DESIRE" TO INJURE

"Desire" to injure presents a problem very similar to the problem of obedience and aggression. Let us consider a situation where a person engages in a behavior that he knows is quite dangerous to another person, not because he "wishes" to inflict injury upon the second person, but simply because the latter is in his way and constitutes a barrier to goal attainment. Such behaviors are often called "instrumental aggression." It may be inaccurate to argue that there is a "desire" to injure, but it is certainly accurate to maintain that the person committing this act had a fair expectation that it might result in injury to the other.

INFLICTING HURT IN ORDER TO HELP

Finally, we certainly do not wish to accuse the surgeon of aggressive behavior toward his patients, even though he does on occasion inflict pain and injury upon them. We shall assume, again keeping in mind the possibility of rare exceptions, that the surgeon acts in order to bestow upon the patient a benefit greater than the initial injury inflicted. In general, where a behavioral readiness and an expectation envisage a greater good than harm, our definition of aggression will be deemed inapplicable.

"AGGRESSION" AS A MEANINGFUL TERM

These examples should make it quite clear that considerable disagreement exists in what even experts call "aggression." It follows that if there is disagreement about defining observed events as "aggressive" or otherwise, we cannot hope to study the *determinants* of aggression or, more precisely, the *relationships* governing the occurrence of aggressive behavior. It should be clear by now that when we claim to observe an act of "aggression," we do more than describe an observed event; we make an inference about an inner state within the aggressor—a state that could loosely be called "intention," "desire to inflict injury," and so forth. In other words, we infer an unobservable state, or a *construct,* from our observation.

The absence of constructs in a science would make any kind of theory, and even the simplest prediction, impossible. In psychology, too, an assumption of a causal, lawful relationship implies an orderly series of states within the organism which produces behavior in an orderly fashion. For instance, if rats are found to run at speed x after having been deprived of food for 4 hours, and at speed y after 16 hours, it would make no sense at all to predict running speed after 11 hours of deprivation unless we assume that deprivation (or perhaps artificially produced reduction in blood sugar) produces, in an orderly, predictable fashion, an inner state which, in turn, stands in an orderly relationship with running, consummatory, and other behaviors, and which we may call "hunger." The construct is thus validated by the orderliness with which more than one antecedent condition is related to *more than one* behavior.

To cite another example: there are various ways in which we can make a rat "afraid" of a certain locale or stimulus. That is, after the rat has experienced some aversive event at that locale or in contiguity with that stimulus, it will then learn a variety of tasks in order to avoid that situation, such as turning a wheel or pressing a bar (Miller, 1948). Without in any way interpreting the animal's response in human terms, it is quite legitimate to speak of an inner state, produced by various means, having the property of motivating the animal to escape the situation. Scientific rigor is not endangered by calling this state "fear."

In both cases, that of "hunger" and that of "fear," these constructs are inferred from unequivocal behaviors to which they give rise and from the events that precede them. Considerable difficulties, however, have arisen in the definition of constructs applicable to the complex situations of interpersonal behavior. In the case of the term "aggression," a great variety of behaviors—from words spoken in a certain manner to pushing death-producing buttons (which may look no different from bell buttons)—have been called "aggressive" because they allegedly are caused by some "aggressive tendency." This alleged inner state is then, in turn, inferred from the same behaviors which, without it, might have no "aggressive" connotation. The circularity of this reasoning should be painfully obvious.

This is not to say that the construct "aggressive tendency" is inherently worthless. If we can specify various antecedent conditions that produce one of several possible behaviors in an orderly and predictable fashion, then the construct of "intent to aggress" may acquire the same usefulness in theorizing as the construct of "hunger." The important point is that any construct must be inferrable, not only by the responses which it supposedly generates (for this makes the whole argument clearly circular), but by testable predictions of other, as yet unobserved, behaviors. It makes no sense to say "the animal is hungry because it is eating," for it could be said with equal plausibility that "the animal is eating because it is hungry." The term "hungry," which refers to an unobservable, *inferred* state, acquires usefulness only if, on the one hand, we tie it in to various antecedent events, such as deprivation, glucose injections, and so on, and on the other, predict not only that the animal will now eat a certain amount, but also that it will work for food, display agitation, and so on, and that these behaviors subside after eating.

Similarly, "aggressive tendency," or "intent," cannot usefully be inferred from a single observed behavior. (We often do this in practice, but in that case we really take for granted a number of assumptions, such as "I know *from past experience* that socking someone on the chin is *one of the behaviors* from which it is reasonable to infer 'intent to injure.' ") In order for the constructs to have any value in the framework of empirical psychology, we must be able to specify a number of antecedent events (thwarting, deprivation, insult, etc.) that produce predictable amounts of one or more of several behaviors (striking, shouting, stabbing).

The concept of "intent" as a construct, then, should not, in principle, trouble us, even though some psychologists have argued that it is illegitimate to consider anything but observable events. There is ample precedent for such constructs; in fact, they could be maintained to be indispensable for theory construction.

We could, therefore, define "aggressive intent" as the tendency to engage in an act perceived as leading to a goal state that involves injury to another person. The term "involves" means that the aggressor has *some* expectation of actually inflicting the injury. The definition is not synonymous with "aggression" itself, for not only the behavioral readiness but also the expectation of aggressing successfully can be inferred from observations *other* than the aggressive behavior.

There is, however, one shortcoming inherent in the construct "intent": it is usually conceived as a qualitative, all-or-none term. We have chosen the term "expectation" in preference to "intent." It does *not* mean that the aggressor "wishes" to inflict injury, or that he is *certain* of doing so, but only that he does *not* expect with absolute certainty that his aggressive act will fail. We can say that he has an expectation greater than zero that his aggressive act will result in injury. In addition, the term "expectation" more properly encompasses situations where injury, although not the main goal of an act, is a side effect apt to occur with some degree of probability—as, for instance, in instrumental aggression—without being, at least in the usual meaning of the term, "intended" by the aggressor.

This assumption of purposive or rule-following model in human, even some animal, behavior is not a new one (Tolman, 1932; Miller, Galanter, & Pribram, 1960); but it is surprising how often psychologists in the so-called softer areas of psychology resist its adoption. Peters (1960) makes an important distinction between causal and rule-following explanations of behavior. The first may serve to explain the types of acts a person is impelled or "driven" to do, and generally corresponds to a stimulus-response paradigm, as well as Freudian unconscious motivation. But, Peters argues, such a model is really inadequate to explain the bulk of human behavior, which consists in *selecting* from a wide variety of behaviors having a specific anticipated end effect. When a person strokes his chin, he may be suffering from an itch (causal explanation); or he may wish to convey an impression of thoughtful deliberation, and believes that his gesture will make him appear in the desired light (rule-following explanation).

Similarly, the causal model may be adequate to explain certain rage states or temper tantrums at an early stage in life, and account for "moving about in an agitated fashion." But when we consider the often subtle and tortuous ways of human aggression, we must clearly assume a knowledge of means-end states, or of "what action produces what outcome." Even though the perpetrator may not be certain that the contemplated act will achieve the desired end, he must have some expectation of success.

A DEFINITION OF "AGGRESSION"

The preceding arguments would seem to imply the following stipulations. In order for a behavior to be classified as "aggressive"—

1. It must be transitive; that is, directed against a living target (as opposed to being purely autistic).
2. The attacker must have an expectation or subjective probability greater than zero of reaching the object and of imparting a

noxious stimulus to it, or both. (No stipulation is made that the target could not also be the attacker himself.)

At this point, it might be asked why the definition includes no affective or physiological arousal component. Clearly, people sometimes "fume with desire" to injure another person, and rejoice at perceiving his injury. However, such an arousal state is neither necessary nor sufficient to infer aggressive intent. A person may commit atrocities in cold blood, or, conversely, he may passionately wish another person harm, without being able (or even wanting) to do anything about it.

PERSONALITY CHARACTERISTICS IN READINESS TO AGGRESS

As yet, nothing has been said about some very relevant aspects of aggression. Our definition makes no distinction between a person who is disposed or "primed" to commit or advocate aggression at the slightest provocation and one who has a "high threshold" for such behaviors. For the latter case, the phrase "slow to anger" comes to mind; but "anger," as it is commonly used, implies some emotional state. However, the harsh individual described above may be readily induced to mete out pain and injury, not because he is consumed with rage, but because he has learned that his parents, tradition, or his peer group advocate such harshness. The personality characteristic, response style, or habit, which we shall call "hostility," thus differs from what we propose to define as "aggression," because aggression is a class of behaviors, whereas hostility is not. In terms of this definition, then, it makes no sense to say "X acted in a hostile manner," for hostility does not refer to behaviors. More properly, we should say "X acted in such a manner as to allow us to infer a hostile disposition." When we speak of a person as being "hostile," we think of him as one who has a habit of or propensity for disliking others, wishing them harm or aggressing against them. His negative tendencies may extend to political, religious, and other concepts, but apparently only when such concepts attach to or originate from people, so that attack upon the concepts becomes attack against, or injury wished upon, these people. The construct is therefore not equivalent to the expectation inherent in an aggressive act; for such expectation refers to specific situations and involves perceptions of means-end states, whereas hostility refers to a more general predisposition. To make the distinction still clearer, we can easily conceive of a very hostile person who is unconcerned with aggression at a given point in time, and of an individual ranking very low on habitual hostility engaging in an aggressive act. On the other hand, it is not argued that hostility and aggression are unrelated. Some of these possible relationships (not necessarily causal) will be discussed later.

Anger will be an important topic in later arguments, and we shall attempt to show that it plays several parts in behavior. But at this point, a useful definition is of value because, again, it will differ from earlier, and vaguer, definitions. Let us, then, define "anger" as a "physiological arousal state coexisting with fantasied or intended acts culminating in harmful effects of another person."

This definition of "anger" may appear cumbersome and farfetched, but it is no longer a source of confusion. Anger may indeed be present without the *expectation* of inflicting injury, and without behaviors directed to such an end. By this definition, a person may aggress without being angry, and he may be angry without aggressing. On the other hand, we believe it makes no sense to speak of "anger" merely to designate emotional behavior, without some evidence that it is accomplished either by (possibly unfulfillable) fantasies of hurting another, or by plans to do so. This definition, it will be noted, implies cognitive processes of some complexity and therefore excludes most animals and very small children. A tiger's emotional behavior preparatory to attack is thus not considered anger, nor is the temper tantrum of the nonverbal infant.

In order to keep the definition from being even more intricate, we have omitted the case where a person is emotionally aroused and fantasies or plans injury, but does so in order to obtain sexual rewards. Sexual sadism will not be considered anger.

With these definitions of aggression, hostility, and anger we can now look at situations of harmful or beneficial interpersonal behavior.

II

Homo Homini Lupus: The Aggressive Instinct, Thanatos, and Other Myths

"Aggressive instinct" is a catchy phrase, but its usefulness for an understanding of interpersonal aggression is quite limited. Nor is it very useful to compare animals fighting or killing for prey with the complex human phenomena that constitute the bulk of aggression within and across societies.

*W*HEN VIOLENCE COMMITTED by one human being (or even an animal) comes up in a discussion, it is frequently suggested that the deplorable event occurred because man possesses a "natural" instinct for aggression—an instinct, moreover, that is universal in nature, and can be detected in some form or other in all animal species. By analogy, it could even be argued that some plants also possess aggressive instinct because they sometimes crowd out other plants, thereby causing them to perish. (Incidentally, it is a curious paradox that often the very same people who shudder whenever comparisons are drawn between animals and man in the areas of, say, learning or physiology, will pontificate on the unchangeable nature of "base" instincts in man.)

The concept of aggressive instinct is not new. The English philosopher Thomas Hobbes, author of the well-known political treatise *Leviathan,* coined the phrase *Homo homini lupus*—"Man is [like] a wolf to [his fellow] man." He meant by this that man possessed—or is possessed by—an overriding cruelty toward his fellowman, unrelieved by consideration or compassion. McDougall, who in 1908 wrote the first book that used the term "Social Psychology," speaks of an "instinct of pugnacity."

13

FREUD'S THEORY OF THE AGGRESSIVE INSTINCT

Other thinkers discussed the tragedy of life in various forms and generally agreed that this aggressive instinct is indeed a terrible scourge. Sometimes their despair would be relieved by the hope for a wholly peaceful hereafter in which sheep and lion would lie down side by side (together, presumably, with Communists and Liberals). It was Sigmund Freud, however, who first examined the psychological aspects of aggression, and the driving force behind it. In his earlier works (1909–1919) he viewed aggression as a variant or displacement of the energy, or the libido, that activates living organisms. This concept, of course, implies that the variant can, at least ideally, be prevented from occurring by directing the libido into creative rather than destructive channels. But later on, Freud's view changed, and he expressed his philosophical pessimism[1] in his announcement that life consists of an eternal conflict between two animating forces: a creative, or growth, force, which he named Eros (the name of the Greek god of love), and a destructive force, which he named Thanatos, or Death (1920). From the moment of its inception, he argued, any living organism carries within itself the source of its own destruction. Thanatos, feeble at first, but indubitably present, immediately begins to drive the organism back toward its earlier, inert, and undifferentiated form. Its effects are not confined to its own host; as organisms strive to mate and procreate, and just as friendship or altruism represent variants of Eros, Thanatos will invariably be present in these and other relations among organisms.

It is true that Freud expressed the hope that human reason could eventually counterbalance the most destructive and pointless expressions of this deadly force. But at the same time, it follows clearly from Freud's argument that the drive to kill and destroy is an integral and inseparable part of life; some redirecting of the force against less objectionable targets may be possible, but it can never be abolished. Also, any imposition of force or restraint upon an organism—for instance, the necessary limits imposed by any form of society upon the immediate fulfillment of any craving—inevitably activates the destructive force, with the result that wars, violence, and even violence against the self (exemplified by neurotic disorders and suicide), develop.

LORENZ' THEORY OF THE AGGRESSIVE INSTINCT

Konrad Lorenz, generally considered the father of ethology, or the study of life in its natural habitat, wrote a book in 1963 which he called *Das Sogenannte Böse* (*The So-Called Evil*), recently translated under the

[1] The meaning of "pessimism" as it is used here is rather remote from the meaning implied in everyday usage.

title *On Aggression* (1966). Lorenz belongs to the regrettably small group of scientists whose writings are a literary delight, and his descriptions of animal behaviors represent invaluable extensions of our knowledge. But our concern lies with some of his inferences and generalizations about what he considers the many interacting instincts that constitute life. Of these, he views the aggressive instinct as a major and indispensable one. Survival and evolution could not occur if organisms had no provisions for protecting their territory against intrusion, for defending their young, and for engaging in contests in order to select their strongest specimens for procreating. This force, or drive, is an inevitable component of life. Moreover, instincts must find periodic outlets; otherwise, the force behind them would increase without limit. Lorenz (1966, pp. 209 ff.) strongly argues the point that man suffers from an insufficient discharge of a high aggressive drive. He maintains that emotion has long and wrongly been considered a villain in that it, rather than reason, is alleged to be the great enemy of the survival of mankind. On the contrary, he says, imagine a person possessed of no emotions at all; just pure reason. Such a person would view the utmost horrors—even the very destruction of the world—with no emotional involvement at all. Reason, Lorenz asserts, is a later development in man; and it is the earlier, more basic, instincts that make him capable of love, friendship, feeling, appreciation of beauty, creativity, curiosity, and so on.[2] He gives examples of guilt or moral responsibility in animals that seem to react with strong feelings of guilt or regret over having injured either a member of their own species, or even over having committed some very minor misdemeanor.

To buttress his argument, Lorenz points to the essential paradox of the doctrine of morality by Kant. According to Kant, we owe less gratitude to a sincerely benevolent man than to a person who does a good deed simply because it is the right, just, and moral thing to do, even though he acts reluctantly, and perhaps even dislikes the beneficiary. Yet normally, Lorenz points out, we do the very opposite. When someone does us a favor, we examine his motives, and cherish his deed most if we perceive it to originate from what we call genuine or spontaneous kindness. If we have the impression that he dislikes us intensely and yet acts kindly toward us, we tend not to admire him for it. Indeed, this kind of behavior reminds us painfully of the bigoted, sanctimonious hypocrite who, having no capacity for kindness or warmth, treats others with contempt and humiliating generosity. Thus, we "instinctively" cherish emotion over reason.

---

[2] Lorenz' argument could, of course, be very easily turned upside down by the invitation to contemplate a human being totally devoid of reason. His assertion is questionable on philosophical grounds also. Stoicism, for instance, maintains plausibly that the absence of emotional involvement enables man to attain high virtue. However, since it is not my purpose to discredit emotion, I shall not pursue this line of argument further.

In another attack on the evils of civilization, Lorenz also argues that the crowding that occurs in a sophisticated society implies one's having to distribute one's positive personal feelings over too many others, for too much of the time, thereby impoverishing the strength of the personal bond and increasing the aggressive drive. He adduces anecdotal evidence to the effect that, within species, aggression in most animals is apparently counteracted by inhibition, which stops a victor from killing his opponent after defeating him. Man, however, has lost this inhibition; it has become ineffective because most human slaughter occurs at such a distance that the victim's "posture of submission," which triggers inhibitions against killing, is not seen by the aggressor.

Unfortunately, there are no easy solutions to this dilemma. For instance, it would not do simply to repress the aggressive instinct indiscriminately, for there exist important distinctions among various cultures. For instance, the entire social system of the Bornean headhunters would fall apart if they were prevented from hunting heads. Thus we cannot be sure which values (or norms) are those that deserve survival, as opposed to those that we must in some way, even at some cost or risk, try to overcome. Lorenz gives another example—that of a juvenile gang, which has a social structure very similar to that of primitive human groups, filling basic instinctual needs. Finally, Lorenz argues that "militant enthusiasm" can be elicited with the predictability of a reflex when the following environmental situations arise: First of all, the social unit with which the subject identifies himself must appear to be threatened by some danger from the outside. That which is threatened may be a group of people unified by some common attribute or interest, a family, a little community of close friends, or it may be a larger social unit (a tribe or nation, for example) held together and symbolized by its own specific social norms and rights. As the larger social unit assumes the character of autonomous values, it can, quite by itself, represent the object in whose defense militant enthusiasm can be elicited, and men follow the call to arms, to battle for their "self-evident" truths. From all this it follows that this response can be brought into play in such a manner that extremely different objects, ranging from the sports club to the nation, or from the most obsolete mannerisms or ceremonials to the ideal of "scientific truth" or of the "incorruptibility of justice," can produce such militant enthusiasm, And, of course, the prototype of "militant enthusiasm" is militarism itself.

The second key stimulus that contributes to the releasing of "militant enthusiasm" is hatred for the enemy who threatens the values mentioned above. This enemy too can be of a concrete or an abstract nature: it can be a specific attacker, or Jews or Huns or Boches, and even more abstract concepts such as world capitalism, bolshevism, or fascism.

In other words, whereas Freud stresses the negative aspects of the destructive drive, Lorenz argues, with considerable cogency, that there could be no life without conflict, even death. Both writers, however, see aggression as a universal, biological instinct.

SOME OBJECTIONS TO LORENZ' THEORY

Lorenz attempts to draw bold inferences about complex human behaviors from his ethological studies, with perplexing results. For instance, he illustrates his claim for the need of accumulated aggressive instinct to find an outlet, with an anecdote about an old aunt whose initial affection for her maidservants invariably changed to strong resentment and hostility.

The remedies Lorenz suggests are feeble. He proposes a "draining off" of aggressive drive through friendly competition. But this prescription leads to the inference that people and nations engaged in competitive sports would be less aggressive than others. One is at a loss, however, to find even anecdotal evidence that such activities distinguish combative from peace-loving peoples. Indeed, one suspects that if sports were ever seen as diminishing a nation's warlike spirit, athletics would be quickly equated with high treason, especially in countries bent upon conquest and expansion.

On occasion, Lorenz seems bewildered by his own analogies. As was pointed out a little earlier, he argues that we have no immediate knowledge of the function and/or survival value of the majority of our established customs, but at the same time he views them as almost sacred. Also, he concedes that human ritual is not hereditarily or genetically transmitted, but has to be learned from generation to generation (and, we might add, within specific social contexts). Nevertheless, he insists that the parallel between instinctive animal behavior and human rituals is strong enough so that reasonable analogies may be drawn.

It is difficult to take issue with Lorenz' contention that "within-species aggression" constitutes mankind's greatest threat; antediluvian monsters or army ants are unlikely to bring about mankind's doom. But his admonition that the inhibition against killing occasionally observed in animals is largely absent in man, because in the case of man the victim is usually too far away to present the stimuli for inhibition to the aggressor, presents a paradox: if the stimulus is too remote to elicit inhibition, how can it elicit aggression? Also, history provides some lusty instances of mayhem and extermination at close quarters, with inhibition nowhere in evidence.

Furthermore, it is not plausible to compare aggressive drive and hunger drive, as Lorenz does. The former cannot be shown to be a function of "deprivation," or time elapsed since the last aggressive act was committed; whereas hunger depends, in an orderly and often observed manner, upon the length of the preceding fast.

The spurious nature of Lorenz' analogies becomes obvious if we consider, say, hoarding by squirrels and humans. In the former case, we are dealing with a universal characteristic of the species, and can point to its specific survival value. When we encounter hoarding by a miser, however, we are, first of all, not observing a behavior that is present in the entire human species, and are rarely able to discover any survival value in that behavior. We could, of course, argue that all humans have a hoarding instinct, but that it is easily superseded by other, learned, behaviors. But this "explanation" would be of little value in deciding why some people hoard and others do not, or why *some* people hoard *some* things *some* of the time. It might be argued, then, that Lorenz introduces a fundamental confusion between instinctive behaviors and behaviors which, whatever their earliest or basic origins, have now become so modified by individual experiences—that is, by learning—that it just no longer makes any sense to look for instinct-specific antecedents.

There is another objection to Lorenz' position: he fails to discuss any of the relationships between behavior and physiological events, which have been the subject of numerous studies over the past few decades—studies in which some very interesting relationships have been found. For instance, fighting behavior in mice has been shown to depend on the concentration of the male hormone testosterone (Beach, 1945; Beeman, 1947). Scott and Fredericson (1951, p. 240) found that even in the relatively primitive mammals such as mice and rats the acquisition of fighting habits depends on hormonal factors, but that the *habit* of fighting after, say, frustration depends chiefly upon previous learning.

Quite early studies showed that the cortex apparently exerts a controlling or inhibiting influence on diffuse, ragelike behavior (Cannon & Britton, 1927; Bard & Rioch, 1937). Somewhat more recently, Bard and Mountcastle (1947), Schreiner and Kling (1956), and Brady (1960) showed that different portions of the brainstem function as generators and inhibitors of emotional arousal related to attack behavior.

We now also know that attack or fighting behavior in animals depends upon a mechanism fundamentally different from that proposed by "instinct" theorists. Wasman and Flynn (1962) found that electric stimulation of certain portions of a cat's hypothalamus (a small part of the brainstem) produces well-coordinated attack. They further found apparent differences in "defensive fighting," such as might be observed when an animal's young or its territory is to be protected, and in "stalking" behavior, aimed at killing an edible animal. But the probability of such attack varies also with the environmental stimulus situation, and is less likely to occur when no "suitable" object of attack is visible (Levison & Flynn, 1965). Thus it is internal and external stimulation, and not the accumulation of dammed-up energy, that leads to attack.

Some very recent studies indicate that in the human male an abnor nal complement of chromosomes may result in below average intelligence, poor self-control, and a propensity for violence. (The prime suspect in he slaying of eight nurses in Chicago, Richard Speck, is an instance n point.) Here, again, we must view this finding in the proper context. First of all, by far the greatest part of violence is committed by biologically normal individuals. Secondly, even the men so afflicted do not necessarily become mass murderers. Their cases, no less than any other, require a careful study of their individual experiences and the cultural tradition they assimilated, however distortedly. After all, it may well be that men with such an abnormal chromosome structure are capable of normal, lawful lives.

It should, perhaps, be stressed once more that we do not for a moment deny that there exist enormous individual differences in temperament, arousability, and self-control. Undoubtedly, our genetic heritage contains determinants of such generic psychological attributes, especially since they are closely related to the functioning of the nervous system, including some highly specialized areas in the brain. Surely, no one can take issue with the argument that our self-examination, as members of this threatened species, should include an understanding of our biological attributes. In some instances, we shall find that such attributes, and their concomitant psychological tendencies, greatly enhance the likelihood of certain behaviors. But, again, these behaviors do not occur in a vacuum and they are not rigidly tied to a specific stimulus configuration. The task of the psychologist seeking to understand the behavior of man toward his fellowman has been enriched, and perhaps complicated, by additional variables. It is senseless to argue that it has been rendered irrelevant or redundant.

The chief objection to "instinct" theories is not that they deny possible innate, genetically determined tendencies but, rather, that they constitute, at least theoretically, a terminal position that reverentially accepts the state of the world and offers no systematic prescription for discovering causal relationships.

The concept of "instinct" may at first sight be appealing in that it implies proper respect before the creation, but upon closer inspection it turns out to be quite sterile. It explains nothing and provides no new information; only a new term for observation. When a given event is observed, it is ascribed to the instinct; when it is absent, the "instinct" is deemed to be lacking.[3] This position is by definition alien to the scientific

Lest these remarks be construed as a derogation of McDougall's (1908) remarkable work, let it be emphasized that McDougall's "instincts" are really more similar to "drive states" (Miller, 1959). Therefore, although they are thereby not necessarily invested with the the mantle of truth, McDougall cannot be accused of simplicistic thinking. Indeed, he himself attacks those who ascribe every observed behavior to a pertinent instinct.

method. The conflict is not merely one of doctrine. As we have seen, the scientist's dissatisfaction with such hieratic pronouncements has been highly fruitful in just that area of aggression which theorists had conceded to the domain of imponderable mystery.

The findings stressing stimulus variables as opposed to genetically transmitted aggressive mechanisms are in no way to be seen as a "simplification" of nature. Nothing that is said here detracts in any way from the admirable complexity of living organisms. To say that attack is the result of specific stimulations and the intactness of certain brain centers, and not of the accumulation of a drive, is in no sense a "simplified" explanation; indeed it is this flexibility, the capacity for individual learning, which is the most important evolutionary advance. But such a theory leads to quite different predictions: the drive or instinct theory predicts periodic outbursts of attack, even where no outside stimulation is present; the stimulation theory implies that certain stimuli are necessary for attack to occur. Moreover, the importance of individual experience or learning discovered in the last two decades extends not only to man but to lower mammals, perhaps even to birds. It is not disputed that almost every species of animal can be shown to attack, not members of their own species exclusively, but also members of other species. There can be little doubt that fighting, aggressing, killing, and maiming are an integral part of the history of life. Indeed, it takes only very simple arithmetic to see that if animal did not kill animal, the earth would be overpopulated by many different species within a very short period of time. Animals kill to live, and sometimes killing to live does not simply mean killing for food; it may mean killing in order to preserve certain territorial needs, or to secure or retain a mate. And sometimes even in animals, what might be called wanton cruelty can be observed, in which killing occurs without any motive obvious to the human observing. But we are, after all, concerned with man's behavior toward his fellowman, and must find out empirically the usefulness of certain formulations toward its prediction and control.

In considering these interpretations of complex human behavior in terms of mysterious forces and farfetched analogies, one is struck by the conceptual acrobatics upon which they are based. This should not be ascribed to the author's simplemindedness. Very often it is the daring conceptual leap that leads to unsuspected discoveries. At other times—and this is perhaps especially true of Freud—original texts have been interpreted and quoted out of context to such an extent that a brilliant speculation may appear as trite assertion. However, whether through the author's intention, or through subsequent distortions, it often happens that these interpretations acquire a surprising similarity to the mythical explanations used by ancient or primitive peoples to account for unusual or threatening events for which no observable cause could be found

Because myths apparently are not restricted to peoples remote from us in time or sophistication, a short excursion into the history and meanings of the concept "myth" is in order.

MEANINGS OF MYTH

Originally, "myth" referred to a legend or a fable postulating a causal relationship between an unnatural or supernatural being and an observed event, usually of crucial nature (Frazer, 1935; Cassirer, 1944; Malinowski, 1936). These events affect a society either collectively, as in a flood or famine, or individually, as would be the case for birth, illness, and death. Through tradition, these beliefs acquired social sanction as valid as that accorded to the daily actions of survival and interpersonal exchanges.

By definition, such a relationship lay outside the realm of systematic and factual inquiry. In the views of Frazer (1935) and, in a more detailed form, of Malinowski (1936) the function of this type of myth was primarily to fill the void caused by man's powerlessness in the face of unexplainable and mysterious occurrences. Greek and oriental myths, as well as many of those related in the Old Testament, are primarily in this class. In addition, myths sometimes serve not so much to deal with crises in which man finds himself impotent as to enhance his capabilities beyond the humanly possible. Germanic myths seem to fall primarily into this category, although a good case could be made for the *Iliad*. More modern instances that come to mind are those of Faust and Superman. This function of myth is highly relevant to a discussion of prejudice, and will be dealt with later on.

The persistence of such beliefs in a sophisticated society is at first sight surprising. But a crisis of knowledge can also occur when a sophisticated society, not susceptible to rain dances and voodoo, finds that certain occurrences cannot be accomodated by the current state of knowledge. Cassirer (1946) expresses astonishment that the prevalence of myths in Western societies is restricted to political (and we might add, social) areas; but this state of affairs can be easily explained: not long ago, the biological sciences were pervaded by myths accounting for our inadequate knowledge of heredity and the microorganism which produces disease. Even the phlogiston theory[4] was accepted until less than 200 years ago. Today, we are highly advanced in the physical and natural sciences, and should expect little need for mythical explanations in those areas. In the social sciences the situation is somewhat different: granted that

---

As the reader will recall, the phlogiston theory asserted that combustible materials contained a substance, called phlogiston, which became liberated in the process of combustion.

LIBRARY ST. MARY'S COLLEGE

our knowledge has advanced considerably in this century, it has not kept up with the even faster growth of problems with which it must deal, and which arise partly from population growth and partly from the same rapid progress in the physical and biological sciences which has made myths in those areas obsolete.

The actual and potential threat that man constitutes for his fellow-man presents a problem whose solution we have not yet begun to discover. It is no wonder that this state of affairs may engender a sense of impotence and helplessness very similar to that of an aborigine viewing a lunar eclipse and interpreting it as the ingestion of the moon by an enormous beast. The mythical explanation eliminated intense uncertainty, a state that many psychological findings have shown to be unpleasant (Berlyne, 1960; Festinger, 1957).

There is, however, yet another mechanism, whereby myths or magical thinking may become part of the cognitive repertory of a fairly sophisticated society. Cassirer (1944) views myth, not as a mark of helplessness or fear, but as both a precursor and a persistent component of religion. Thus it originates not so much from man's desire to understand and control nature as from his desire to be an integral, a sentient, and, in Frazer's terminology, a "sympathetic" part of it. He also considers myth as a form of poetry: mythical beings and events are the result, not of primitive man's simplemindedness, but of his deep empathy with, and glorification of, nature. Sarbin (1968) offers some interesting ideas about how an originally poetic metaphor may come to be accepted as literal fact. His attack is directed against the alleged "state" of anxiety which, he asserts, has become a reified entity, or a "thing," in the organism. A striking example of Sarbin's thesis—that the poetic metaphor becomes a factual proposition—is afforded by the connotations of such expressions as "Anger welled up inside him," or "He choked with anger." These expressions may have become transformed into the ethologists' hydraulic model of aggressive instinct, which asserts that aggression resembles an internal fluid whose pressure increases and must be drained off, or catharted, from time to time. Such a shift occurred, for instance, from Lorenz (1937) metaphoric model to that of Tinbergen (1951), which tends to view instinctual energy as literally following hydraulic principles (Hinde 1959).

Further evidence for Sarbin's theory of myth can be derived from a comparison of expressions denoting physiological states in some of the major Indo-Germanic languages. For instance, the quite unexceptionable English version of "I am hungry" admits of two equivalent German translations: "Ich bin hungrig" (I am hungry) and "Ich habe Hunger" (I have hunger). In French and Italian, the shift to the inner "thing" has become complete: "J'ai faim," and "Ho fame" (I have hunger) are the only remaining versions.

It is not necessary, for our purposes, to take a stand in favor of one or another of the theories mentioned above. In fact, it could be reasonably maintained that what we might call Sarbin's "metaphor shift" is more likely to occur in situations of ignorance and powerlessness, which in themselves are generators of myths, rumors, and fantastic speculations.

A belief in myth, as we have seen, may render a complex situation more manageable; at the same time, it commands a singlemindedness and unquestioning commitment that might otherwise be diluted by disputatious examinations of the many sides of an issue. The fanaticism with which a pseudo-Freudian ethos is advocated by an ill-advised coterie of psychoanalysts is a case in point: the outsider is alleged to be incapable of understanding the system, and therefore cannot question it; and the insider, the bonafide member, must accept all interpretations, for to deny would constitute a defensive process.

Such a "closed system," which admits of no critical examination, tends to lead to vague, sterile, and often tautological statements. If we hope to gain a greater understanding of the determinants of man's destructive behavior, we must not allow explanations of aggressive behavior in terms of primeval mystical determinants to shunt aside questions that urgently need answering.

In sum, to argue that aggression is a "universal instinct"—something that everybody is subjected to—allows us to explain and to understand very little. Also, the simple information that some people are extremely aggressive most of the time, whereas others show very little aggression, does not allow us to predict in any manner against whom an aggressor will aggress, and when his "aggressive needs" will be "satisfied." It is not crucial to insist on the a priori assumption that behavior is *infinitely* modifiable through learning. The real question is *"How much* is this behavior modifiable by learning?" Or, "How much do individual experiences matter compared to other contributing factors that are independent of an individual's experience?" That hypothetical portion which is both stereotyped and unmodifiable may not be important enough, as far as human interactions in a complex and developed society are concerned, to contribute significantly to a serious inquiry into the antecedents, the manifestations, and the modification of aggressive behavior.

III

The Frustration-Aggression Hypothesis

This chapter examines the usefulness of the most popular of all "global" theories of aggression. Do we really gain greater understanding—or predictive ability—of where and how aggression will occur by invoking frustration as *the* cause? What do we mean by the term "frustration"? It is suggested here that explanations of aggression in terms of frustration tend to be circular; that is, each of the two terms is cited as evidence for the other. Once that "frustration" is unequivocally defined, we find that its being followed by aggression is more likely to depend upon cultural norms than upon some invariant, innate link. Further, the most abominable instances of aggression are often performed by individuals who are no more frustrated than anyone else.

ONE MORE "GLOBAL" THEORY of aggression remains to be examined before we proceed to a systematic analysis of the antecedents of aggression. In 1939, a book called *Frustration and Aggression* was published by Dollard, Doob, Miller, Mowrer, and Sears. Its main thesis was cited clearly and unequivocally at the very beginning: "Aggression is always a consequence of frustration," and "occurrence of aggressive behavior always presupposes the existence of frustration and, contrariwise, the existence of frustration always leads to some form of aggression." Therefore, a one-to-one relationship between frustration and aggression is postulated. The authors then carefully define "frustration" as follows:. "Frustration is defined as a condition which exists when a goal response suffers interference" (p. 11). In other words, whenever any type of aggressive act occurs, such an act, according to the hypothesis, is always due to some frustration or interference with a goal response the organism has suffered;

24

and conversely, whenever an organism suffers any kind of thwarting or frustration, it will aggress. It should be noted that the authors make *no* assumption about whether this relationship is learned or innate.

It is not difficult to see how this formulation by Dollard and his colleagues meets the need for mastery and understanding, which, as Frazer (1935) and Malinowski (1936) postulate, constitutes a basic determinant of the myth-making process. At the same time, expressions such as "He made me so mad I could have killed him" testify to the plausibility of Sarbin's (1968) hypothesis of the metaphor shift. The Dollard statement, contrary to first impressions, tells us nothing about some primitive, unalterable reaction to being angered. It is a figure of speech expressing the cultural acceptability of (a) construing a given behavior by another person as anger-producing, annoying, or "frustrating," and (b) responding to this interpretation by attacking the offender. In its terse form, however, the figure of speech has come to imply that someone else's behavior is in some objective way "angering," and that aroused anger "naturally" leads to intensely aggressive retaliation.

INITIAL DIFFICULTIES WITH THE HYPOTHESIS

In fact, this strong assertion that aggression follows frustration, and frustration causes aggression soon encountered considerable difficulties. It did not take very profound observation to point out that quite often people, and also animals, are exposed to interference with their goal-directed response and do not display aggressive behavior. True, the authors conceded that such aggression need not always be observable, but they argued that, even though diluted or disguised, it was never destroyed. Also, "aggression" came to be defined very flexibly and included types of aggression such as physical, verbal, fantasied, or implied.

EARLY REFORMULATION

About two years later, one of the original authors therefore reformulated the hypothesis so that the consequent of "observable aggression" was replaced by "an instigation to aggression" (Miller, 1941). This "instigation to aggression" could either be very weak or it could be outweighed by other behavioral habits; in either case, it would be undetectable to the observer.

EXAMINATION AND CRITICISM

Of the two parts of the hypothesis, that which predicts that aggression follows frustration is the more interesting as well as the more plausible one. It will be examined first, leaving some curious implications of the second part until later.

As I have said, the authors go on record as saying that they are not concerned with whether this alleged relationship is an innate or a learned one. They argue quite simply that it does exist. But this is a very difficult position to maintain: if the relationship is an innate one in all organisms, then we are again dealing with a universal characteristic, which should be reliably observable in all organisms, in all circumstances. If, on the other hand, we are dealing with a *learned* relationship, then the question arises why the relationship should be present in all organisms. In that case, should it not be possible that some organisms do *not* learn this one-to-one relationship? If so, we might, then, be well advised to point out just why some people respond to frustration with aggression, and others do not. It should be noted that the assertion that a behavior can be affected by learning does not exclude that its original occurrence was hereditarily determined. But if aggression is a "basic" response to frustration, and alternative responses represent learned modifications, we are justified in demanding some proof of this "natural" response hierarchy.

The second part of the hypothesis leads to the even more amazing inference that by avoiding all frustration, all aggression will be eliminated. Again, no powerful imagination is required to cite instances in which the most brutal and wholesale aggression had no detectable frustration as antecedent; one need only recall the attempted genocide of the Jewish people by the Nazis. Thus one is hard put to find persuasive arguments for the Frustration-Aggression hypothesis as a meaningful explanatory concept, because of two basic problems.

The first problem is one of definition: what exactly is meant by "frustration"? Are we speaking of an objectively observable set of events, or are we considering a hypothetical inner state of the organism? Originally, the term was operationally defined—that is, it was defined in terms of observable events. Any type of interference with some activity—a thwarting of an organism's movements or of its striving toward a goal—was considered frustration. However, it can be argued quite reasonably that objectively similar events might have quite different effects upon different members of the species, or even upon the same organism, depending upon the circumstances in which they occurred. But if this frustration inside the organism then generates an aggressive *tendency,* which, again, is not necessarily identical to the aggressive *behavior* that we should observe, then how do we avoid the accusation of having reasoned in a totally circular manner? Such reasoning might run as follows: "This organism obviously has been frustrated, because it is aggressing. Granted that you cannot tell me how the frustration occurred or what has frustrated it, but it must be there somewhere; otherwise, it would not have aggressed." Or conversely: "This organism must have some aggressive tendency, because I have just frustrated it. You may not have any means at all of detecting this aggressive tendency, but I know it must be there, because frustration has occurred."

Yet it is obvious that human organisms—and even the higher sub-human organisms—respond differentially to frustration, according to their previous history and also to the present situation they encounter. "Frustration," apparently, must mean something more than an objective state of affairs outside the organism; there must also be some evidence that the state of affairs has made some impression upon the organism, and that some change has occurred in the organism. It must feel (to use common parlance) frustrated. Brown and Farber (1951), for instance, redefined the term "frustration" to signify a hypothetical internal arousal response that occurs in certain stimulus situations. This response, which has a large autonomic or emotional component, could then serve in turn as a stimulus for aggressive responses.

It is easy to see why the authors of the Frustration-Aggression hypothesis sought an objective definition of the term "frustration." Then, perhaps even more than now, every effort was made to objectify what heretofore had been a largely "personal" field of knowledge, namely the understanding of goal-striving conflicts and other complex responses. Yet, having placed a barrier before an organism, we cannot be at all sure that we have really "thwarted" it. Evidence for this must come from the organism's own responses. We are, in other words, postulating an inner state, or a construct, inside the organism, called "frustration," and a second one, "readiness to aggress." It is important to remember that when we speak of such constructs we are not assuming that there is a mystical or mythical something in the organism, like "hunger" or "fear" or "frustration," which makes it do certain things. We are using shorthand terms (with or without "surplus meaning"; see MacCorquodale & Meehl, 1948) to account for relationships among antecedent and consequent events that would otherwise be unrelated, and to express a continuous relationship that we have inferred from a few discontinuous, empirically tested data points. We do, in fact, the very same thing when we speak of a physical or any other relationship. Remember, when we say that at temperature x_1 a mercury column is y_1 inches high, and at temperature x_2 the mercury has height y_2, and so on, we are really looking at empirically determined points, but at the same time we go beyond: we infer a continuous function between temperature and expansion of the mercury column. This conceptual leap is, logically speaking, not at all obvious. It becomes plausible and reasonable only if we infer that there is some lawful bond relating temperature to expansion.

There is no objection, in principle, to assuming two separate states within the organism: one that is the result of an antecedent external stimulus situation, and the other that is the result of the first inner state and that in turn leads to some behavioral manifestation. But in order for these two hypothetical constructs to coexist, they must be susceptible to separate and independent definition. This, unfortunately, has not been the case with this particular hypothesis. Let us try to illustrate this shortcoming with a further example.

It is possible to conceive of a person undertaking or approaching a difficult task with two conflicting motives: one might be his desire to achieve something, to do well; the other, his motivation to avoid failure and humiliation. By definition, neither one of these two constructs is observable or measurable in itself, yet it is possible to assess and evaluate both of them separately, as has been shown by various methods (Miller, 1948). It is then possible to go one step beyond, and predict whether the person will approach or avoid the task at hand, and the intensity with which this resultant behavior will occur.

Similarly, we can assess the relationship between, say, intimidating or threatening a person and his defensive, erratic, or other behavior; of course, we can do this only at specific points. We can introduce a very limited number of intensities of the independent variable—annoyance or intimidation—and we can observe (presumably different) degrees of the type of behavior that will result. Ultimately, though, we go beyond the observed points and assert a relationship between, say, intimidation and defensive behavior. It is not argued here that frustration, that is, a particular kind of emotional arousal state produced by thwarting, cannot be independently measured. It is also not argued that a "readiness to commit aggression" cannot, at least in theory, be assessed, even where no aggressive act is completed. In principle, then, the hypothesis is susceptible to empirical and experimental verification; it does not suffer from the shortcomings of instinct or general innate drive models.

However, no reliable way has yet been suggested or discovered to measure the inner state supposedly resulting from "thwarting," independently of the aggressive tendency which it supposedly engenders, and which, it is asserted, need not even lead to overt aggressive behavior.

Thus, if in each case of what we believe to be frustration we must find some evidence of aggression in order to confirm the occurrence of frustration, and if each case of aggression constitutes a post facto case for frustration, then clearly we have increased neither our theoretical understanding nor predictive accuracy.

The second problem is the direct result of the flexibility of the terms used, and bears a resemblance to the difficulties we encountered in the instinct or drive formulations examined in Chapter II. The hypothesis is "global" in that it attempts to cover all possible cases under one conceptual umbrella. Both the antecedent and the consequent term in this equation have, over time, become quite vague and protean, so that almost any antecedent situation that precedes aggression can, by some stretch of the imagination, be considered as frustrating; and conversely, where a frustration has been imposed (at least according to what you and I would consider a frustrating situation), then, even where no aggression is observed, it can always be argued that somehow, somewhere, an aggressive tendency must be present. It is easy to see that this vagueness or flexibility in the model makes it almost totally circular and therefore not very valuable in our understanding or predicting of the antecedents of aggressive behavior.

PAIN AND AGGRESSION

There is considerable evidence of an innate (though not unmodifiable) bond between some unpleasant events and aggression in rats and mice (O'Kelly & Steckle, 1939; Covain, 1949; Tedeschi, Tedeschi, Mucha, Cook, Mattis, & Fellows, 1959). Azrin (1964); Ulrich and Azrin (1962); Azrin, Hutchinson, and Sallery (1964); Azrin and Hutchinson (1963); and Ulrich, Wolff, and Azrin (1964) found within-species and across-species fighting as a function of pain in such various animals as raccoons, snakes, hamsters, opossums, cats, and even monkeys. We also know that it is unsafe to disturb many animals during feeding, or to interfere with their young. These situations could be readily construed as being frustrating by a proponent of the hypothesis.

In order to account for the problem of including "pain" under "thwarting," or interference with a response, Berkowitz[1] has recently announced an ingenious revision of the Frustration-Aggression hypothesis, which encompasses the aggression-eliciting effects of pain. Because it is conceptually difficult to categorize pain as the interruption of either a goal response or a consummatory response, Berkowitz proposes that pain generates aggression not because it is frustration, but that, instead, both frustration *and* pain produce aggression because they both belong to the class of "aversive stimuli." On this basis, Berkowitz asserts that behaviorists, in their efforts to document the modifiability of behavior, were hasty in dismissing the possibility of an innate bond between such an aversive stimulus and subsequent aggression. This admonition cannot be dismissed lightly. There can be no question that animal data, cautiously interpreted, form an important basis for the formulation of at least tentative hypotheses regarding humans.

It is not the purpose of this chapter to argue that some species might not, in the course of time, have developed mechanisms of attack and defense, contingent upon situations that threaten the survival of the

---

[1] Oral communication.

individual or the species. However, in generalizing on human behavior from these findings, several difficulties arise:

1. Human aggression is rarely the outcome of physical pain, food deprivation, or threat to the offspring.
2. Even where such antecedents as pain or food deprivation can be isolated, the response is not a quick, almost reflexlike attack behavior. Instead, complex symbolic processes intervene, which may, or may not, give rise to aggression.
3. It is difficult to see how the most crucial determinant of animal aggression—pain—can be considered a frustration. To do so comes perilously and, it could be argued, fatally close to using the term tautologically.

The arguments advanced here are not based upon the assumption that phenomena and relationship *interpretable* in the terms we have chosen to call "mythical" do not frequently occur. After all, it is precisely the opportunity for such mythical explanations which gives rise to them. Clearly, a myth that is directly contradicted by daily observations would never arise in the first place. Thus it is not difficult to think of instances of frustrated animals or of people lashing out against someone or something. However, when it is clear that a large number of other variables account for the bulk of human aggressive behavior, then comparisons with animal data may make for spurious similarities.

THE NOTION OF CATHARSIS

Also proposed by the authors of the Frustration-Aggression hypothesis is the notion of "catharsis" and "cathartic effect." "Catharsis" is a Greek word meaning "purification," or "cleansing." Its applicability to the Frustration-Aggression hypothesis lies in the corollary that after aggression has occurred, energy has been consumed (catharsis) and aggressive drive should have lessened (cathartic effect). Catharsis, then, is the purging of such a drive or energy, and the cathartic effect is the subsequent lessening of arousability in the face of frustration and of aggressive tendency or aggressive behavior when such arousal does occur. Again, this notion is one that has found wide popular acclaim and has some prima facie plausibility. We do observe that an aggressive act is quite often followed by subsequent relief, almost as if the person were saying to himself: "Gee, I'm glad I let off steam," or, "I just had to get this thing out of my system." In fact, many psychologists and psychiatrists advocate catharsis as a very useful remedy against "building up" mounting intensities of "need to aggress." Frequently, for instance, we observe that a person who is badgered, annoyed, or thwarted in some way becomes angry and commits aggression. After having committed the aggressive act, or (and this is important) after having had an emotional outburst, he may feel better, and show his relief in a variety of ways.

A necessary step, then, in verifying the notion of catharsis and cathartic effect lies in determining whether, after catharsis has occurred, aggression is less intense than before. But even if we do observe what appears to be such a relationship, we must then ask whether it is really of the type asserted by the hypothesis, namely an invariant relationship between aggression, or the alleged draining-off of aggressive energy through catharsis, and subsequent aggression; or whether it is possible that the relationship occurs at times, but can be ascribed more economically to different causes than those asserted by the hypothesis.

Berkowitz (1962, pp. 196 ff.) mentions two types of catharsis and their cathartic effects. The first, traditional type refers to the expression of aggression followed by a decrease in aggressive tendencies. The second interpretation refers to feelings of pleasantness after having performed an aggressive act. However, Berkowitz questions whether this second type of cathartic effect always occurs. The issue, therefore, reduces itself to whether the lessened intensity of a second aggression, or the lesser likelihood of such an act occurring at all, can be best explained in terms of "draining away of aggressive energy." The experimental evidence is ambiguous.

Aggressive behavior has been found to lower subsequent aggression in some instances (Feshbach, 1955; Thibaut, 1950; Thibaut & Coules, 1952), but in others it has produced an increase in aggression (Kenney, 1953; De Charms & Wilkins, 1963).

Feshbach himself (1956) obtained increased aggression in a later experiment, and presented an interesting analysis of the aggression-enhancing or -reducing effects of (aggressive) fantasy behavior. He hypothesized that aggression is cathartic where the subsequent situation is related to the situation involving the aggressive act, but that a second opportunity to aggress should lead to enhanced aggression where the two situations are unrelated.

Stagner (1944) argues that where aggression is the outcome of habitual hostility, no cathartic effect is to be expected; presumably, because greater habit strength develops with repeated aggression, the strength of aggression should *increase* on those grounds. According to Buss (1961, pp. 80 ff.), catharsis should decrease subsequent aggression where anger is present, but increase it in the absence of anger, because in the latter case, cultural inhibition against aggression has been lowered. De Charms and Wilkins (1963) present strong evidence that hostile statements engender subsequent heightened aggression.

The evidence is thus truly conflicting. Aggression enhances or reduces subsequent aggression; aggression committed by a person on behalf of another may serve either as a substitute (Rosenbaum & De Charms, 1960) or as a model (De Charms & Wilkins, 1963) for the latter's subsequent aggression. However, the difficulties inherent in the interpretation of catharsis phenomena do not end here. After all, the cathartic effect may be due to any of the following reasons: (1) a person has "let off steam"; (2) he has aggressed against someone or other; (3) he has *successfully* aggressed against *anyone;* (4) he has successfully aggressed against the annoying person; (5) he has seen the annoying person punished, even by someone else; his cognitive expectations regarding justice are therefore confirmed and his belief in justice is restored; (6) he has simply become physically tired; (7) he has developed "guilt" subsequent to aggression; and, finally, (8) the person believes that, under the circumstances, only a limited amount of aggression is appropriate. None of these explanations represents catharsis proper.

DISPLACEMENT

The term "displacement," introduced by Freud, and widely found in the popular literature, refers to the shifting of an affect and its behavioral correlates from the original object to a substitute object, presumably one that is similar to the original object on certain perceptual or cognitive dimensions. As applied specifically to aggression, the concept has been invoked (by different names) by instinct theorists as well as the authors of the Frustration-Aggression hypothesis.

As originally conceived by the authors of the Frustration-Aggression hypothesis (Dollard et al., 1939; Miller, 1941), a purely perceptual similarity between the principal frustrator and the ultimate victim would lead to aggressive behavior and a "draining off" of aggressive energy. Here, as in the various "instinct" formulations, there is an obvious similarity to the hydraulic model, with "aggressive energy" serving as the fluid.

But the examples of human displacement so often cited in support of the theory are really quite ambiguous. It is true that people sometimes aggress against someone other than the person against whom they would want to aggress, but the reasons for this may be quite different. For instance, as proposed by White and Lippitt (1960), "self-esteem" may be an important variable. The person feels that he should have aggressed against the original target, and feels ashamed or cowardly for not having done so. At the same time, of course, he realizes that the original object would have been too dangerous an object of attack. Therefore, he now selects a new target which, even though a little less dangerous, is in some way "similar" to the original tormentor, and thereby still provides sufficient balm for the aggressor's self-esteem, so that he can persuade himself that he is not an utter coward, and that he has behaved in a manly fashion. This "displacement" interpretation differs fundamentally from that proposed by the Frustration-Aggression hypothesis. The latter assumes an unthinking "pouring out," whose mechanism is analogous over many many species. The former is based upon complex evaluations of the self and its relation to the environment, and is unlikely to be observed in a rat, or even a monkey. Also, the stimulus variables eliciting such "displacement" are rarely classifiable in terms of perceptual similarity to an original instigator. More often, whatever "similarity" can be surmised to exist depends upon complex cognitive comparisons.

To sum up: The Frustration-Aggression hypothesis and its modifications have difficulty defining the two terms. People disagree widely and plausibly on how either "frustration" or "aggression" should be defined. More important, we find that there is really no one-to-one relationship between these two alleged intervening variables at all. Aggression may often occur without any visible or detectable antecedents to frustration, and, conversely, as far as the hypothesized state called "frustration" can be reasonably inferred, other responses are quite effectively learned. Also, a sort of aimless thrashing about on the part of the subject, as opposed to equally primitive responses—such as freezing, running away, or withdrawing—is sometimes construed as "aggression" simply because the organism happens to strike something, perhaps even a living object. It is clearly pointless to construe such behavior as "aggression," because its pattern is no more organized or sophisticated than running away, screaming, or having a primitive kind of a temper tantrum. Hence, even when violent thrashing about results in (accidental) injury to another organism, it makes little sense to call it "aggression." Again, we are going to be left with the observation that unless we have some reasonably reliable way of establishing a relationship between antecedent and consequent events (the consequent events, of course, being "aggression," unequivocally defined), then all the wise and vague assertions about people aggressing because they have undergone certain frustrations are quite devoid of explanatory meaning. If, on the other hand, the often observed contiguity between some experience of thwarting and aggression is simply the result of a person's experience to the effect that aggression pays off in various ways, either by removing an obstacle or by restoring self-esteem, then the issue is more profitably reformulated in terms of how a person learns to deal with his experiences, and to affect his environment.

The argument questioning the usefulness of the Frustration-Aggression hypothesis will not, it is hoped, be taken as an advocacy of frustration, with the justification that it has not been *proved* to lead to aggression. There also can be little argument that although experiencing some frustrations allows the development of important coping responses, some of the thwartings most of us experience from time to time are no more wholesome than some of the tortures inflicted upon suspects and criminals in the past—and, alas, at present. If a child or an adult can be spared needless or maliciously induced suffering, surely this reduction need not be justified by a hoped-for reduction in aggressiveness! We have merely sought to demonstrate that invoking one aspect of "human nature" will further substantial knowledge by very little.

In the final analysis, our concern is really not whether we can, by untiring investigation, discover a "pure" case of frustration-engendered aggression. Instead, our query aims at discovering stronger relationships between clearly defined, observable antecedents of aggression, and aggression itself.

IV

Anger and Aggression

"Anger" is at first sight conceived as an emotional state. But emotion inferred in others entails a different judgment than when it is recognized in oneself: in the latter case it is also perceived as having a cognitive component, or label, whereby the person describes his condition, even if only to himself. Anger and aggression do not necessarily occur together. Anger may have several cognitive and motivational meanings.

VHEN WE SAY A PERSON is "angry," we mean, first of all, that he is upset or emotionally aroused. We base this diagnosis not only upon his statements. It is quite easy to observe that many physiological aspects undergo drastic changes. An angry person may become red in the face, and his breath and heart rate accelerate. He moves about in an agitated fashion. And chances are that whatever behavior he undertakes, aggressive or otherwise, it will take place with greater intensity. However, we clearly cannot equate the presence of anger with subsequent aggression in human interaction. It is not uncommon to find that this type of agitation does not result in violence against another individual, but instead in, say, renewed efforts on a task at which the person has not succeeded previously. Conversely, we shall have considerable opportunity in later chapters to discuss instances in which great violence and cruelty are committed without the physiological symptoms mentioned above.

However, before we proceed to a more precise examination of the relationship between an inner state called "anger" and aggressive or violent behavior, it may be well to examine the notion of "anger" by itself.

ANGER AND EMOTION

It is clear that when we speak of "anger" we are referring, above all, to an emotional state. Emotion, as it is commonly understood, involves, first of all, physiological changes. People are "deliriously happy," "downcast," "disgusted," "anxious," and so on. There is also little doubt tha a great many emotions can be easily differentiated by casual observatio We can tell whether we ourselves are angry or happy, and we can usuall tell when somebody else is either furious or ecstatic.[1]

In addition, these physiological states are largely outside the volur tary control of the person experiencing them. Moreover, one person ma ascribe an emotional state to another without the other's knowing tha he is supposed to be experiencing the emotion! Indeed, one commonl hears "anger" or "joy" ascribed not only to another human being, bu to animals, even though an observer making such a diagnosis would rarel be willing to go so far as to affirm that the animal *recognizes* this stat and is able to describe it to himself. In other words, the "common sense definition of emotion is really of two kinds: when we speak of emotio in ourselves, we refer to certain physiological changes over which w have admittedly little control but of which we are fully aware, and process of thought or deliberation whereby we tell ourselves that we ar feeling "anxious" or "angry." However, when we observe what we ca "emotion" in another organism, human or otherwise, we do not necessaril attribute to the organism the ability—or, where the ability exists, th temporary disposition—to reflect upon or formulate its state of mind we simply observe the physiological changes, as well as certain change in behavior, and attach a name to them. In doing so, we are, then, dispose to ascribe fairly similar emotions to a dog (and even a rat) as t man—even though the grounds for these emotions need not be assume to be the same.

When we engage in this misleading analogy between, say, the be havior preparatory to attack of certain carnivorous animals or birds an that of man, we fail to distinguish between stereotyped manifestation preparatory to attack and the rather sophisticated state in a human bein to which we refer when we say "he is angry" (or, "I am angry"). Th person who is angry normally knows this and does something about i whereas in the animal, bristling of the hair, baring of the fangs, an so on, are inevitable and unchanging accompaniments of specific, complet attack-sequences.[2] The amazing Charles Darwin (1965) and Konra Lorenz (1963) have drawn this analogy and compared human facial ex pressions during the state of rage to those of animals. But we must, agair distinguish between a repertory or potential for the performance of certai

---

[1] Studies have shown, however, that finer discrimination of the emotions of othe achieve accuracy only when based not only upon facial expression, but movement and even a knowledge of environmental conditions (Munn, 1940; Hunt, Cole, Reis, 1958).

[2] Recent studies (Glickman & Schiff, 1967) have shown that in animals, too, a attack sequence can become short-circuited, with certain components dropping ou In these instances, however, the physiological correlates of arousal appear to b absent.

acts, which is for the greater part transmitted genetically, and the innumerable modifications that have occurred in man, living in many cultures and conditions. More important still, in man, what has largely disappeared is the invariance of the stimuli that generally elicit "emotional" responses in animals. In man, then, although the *capability* to experience emotional arousal states is surely innate, expressions denoting anger differ considerably across cultures, and even within cultures, as do the stimuli eliciting such a response pattern. For instance, in humans, baring one's teeth is not always equivalent to anger (even though it sometimes accompanies it). It is not an integral part of either the emotional state of an angry person, or of attack where it occurs. Some angry people snarl, some laugh, some shout, others become menacingly silent.

THEORIES OF EMOTION

According to the James-Lange theory (Mandler, 1962), the psychological states of emotion precede our awareness of them, and therefore they presumably are, in an evolutionary sense, antecedent to awareness of the states themselves. It does not matter how these physiological states are produced in the first place. This may occur through the perception of an external event or stimulus such as seeing a threatening figure or an object of prey, or they may be produced by, say, intensive movements by the organism itself, or by chemical changes within the organism—whether produced artificially or naturally.[3] As Mandler (1962) points out, it is not necessary to subscribe without qualification to James's position (indeed, we shall soon see that it is in many ways an enormous oversimplification), but it is important to acknowledge that James was the first to state clearly that visceral processes are in some way related to emotional behavior. The difficulties with James's theory are listed by Cannon (1929). They are, briefly, the following: (1) There are instances in which either illness or surgery has eliminated sensory feedback from the viscera. According to James, this should, then, eliminate all forms of emotional behavior. The fact is that it does not, especially in adult members of the species. Behaviors that are quite reliably classifiable as "emotional" continue to exist. (2) Visceral events are not differentiated, as would have to be the case if each visceral state corresponded in quality and amount to a kind and degree of a given emotion. (3) The viscera are insensitive, and changes in them are relatively slow. The perception of an emotion should, therefore, occur only some seconds after the perception of the event causing it, and should require a strong impact. We know,

[3] Indeed, one of James's corollaries is that if we can only succeed to produce an appropriate physiological state—for instance, by acting and moving slowly and calmly when we are really "about to feel very agitated"—we can reduce the state of anxiety we would otherwise experience.

however, that this is not so. We can respond to faint cues, and do so rapidly. (4) Finally, another objection is that the artificial production of visceral changes does not produce "true" emotions, as would be predicted from James's theory.

Cannon's alternative, the Emergency theory, proposes that the sensory input is transmitted by the thalamus in the brainstem, both to cognitive centers in the cortex and to the sympathetic nervous system, so that the production of the physiological and the cognitive states can occur "in parallel," or concurrently. This theory seemingly cuts the Gordian knot of the problem. It requires neither Descartes' mystical synchronization of body and mind, which postulated no communication channel between the two, and it does not incur the problem of making one response—say, the *awareness* of one's emotional state—conditional upon the other (in this case, physiological arousal).

However, it was found subsequently that these theories are insufficient to account for the establishment of emotional behavior. For instance, Wynne and Solomon (1955) showed that dogs whose afferent nerves had been impaired or partially blocked took much longer to learn an avoidance,—that is, a "fear" response—to intense shock than did intact animals. However, when a fear response had become established in intact animals, they continued to behave "fearfully" in the situation, even after neural impairment. That is, they continued to behave "normally" by avoiding the situation before the onset of shock, even though their autonomic nervous system was no longer able to signal to the cortex the visceral components of "fear." Clinical observation in humans with defective nervous systems also shows that a person who is congenitally deprived of experiencing visceral stimulation seems unable to learn how to give appropriate emotional responses. On the other hand, people whose nervous systems become impaired later in life, in the sense that no sensory feedback from the viscera reaches the brain, nevertheless manage to emit, manifest and perceive appropriate emotions. James, therefore, seems to have been partially right: Visceral feedback is necessary to *establish* emotional behavior, but not to *maintain* it. Moreover, these visceral events need not be highly differentiated; they simply need to be present, in a manner of speaking, as a catalyst facilitating the establishment of the emotional repertoire.

COGNITION AND EMOTION

Finally, such visceral events are not in themselves *sufficient;* they must be accompanied by other environmental stimulus conditions. The most convincing demonstration of this theory is given by a study of Schachter and Singer (1962). It showed that physiological arousal produced artificially (by means of an injection)—and, moreover, produced in such a manner that the subjects could not account to themselves for this arousal state—made them very susceptible to "labeling" this state in some cognitive way. When they observed another person (a confederate) behaving "angrily," they themselves behaved in an angry fashion; when they observed the other person behaving exuberantly, they tended to imitate him. The model's behavior had become a clue for the behavior the situation required by "explaining," to the subject, the "reason" for his inner state. On the other hand, the modeling behavior of the other person had considerably less effect when no physiological arousal states had been artificially produced. Another experiment by Schachter and Wheeler (1962) showed that the degree to which subjects experienced amusement at a slapstick movie depended upon the degree of physiological arousal that was present in them. Where a depressant had been administered, very little amusement was shown. A placebo produced moderate amusement; and physiological arousal, artificially produced, led to the greatest state of merriment.

These findings suggest that people do not simply pretend to enact their emotions (except when they are deliberately acting). In order to produce emotional behavior, physiological arousal must be present, unless one has already learned in the past that a given emotion is appropriate in that situation. In a sophisticated human adult, physiological arousal is often experienced without a "reason" for emotion, and therefore without experiencing or manifesting that emotion. For instance, if a person has been running rapidly, he does not afterwards become exuberant, or angry, simply because a physiological change has been produced. It is necessary that the changes observed should be unusual ones, in the sense that they cannot be explained in any customary way. When this arousal state is perceived, a need arises to ascribe it to some cause or to identify it in some way. The behavior of another person may serve as just such a clue. Another person's anger may indicate that this is indeed a situation in which it is "appropriate" to be angry.

The work of Schachter and his associates further supports the theory in that the *type* of physiological arousal for such highly different emotions as anger and exuberance does not have to differ. Its presence, and an opportunity for labeling, are sufficient to produce a given emotional state. On the other hand, as we have said, perception of, say, an angry model, in itself, is not enough; where it is unaccompanied by physiological arousal, the "emotion" will not be perceived or expressed.[4]

We can also think of everyday examples that exemplify this situation. Let us assume that we are in a dark and lonely street, and somebody touches us on the shoulder, from behind. We may experience an immediate

---

[4] We are not concerned here with the phenomena of suggestibility and suggestion, where one person may emulate the physiological state *and* the behavior of another.

emotion of fear, but when we turn around and see an old friend smiling at us, we may suddenly find ourselves laughing and expressing joy with a degree of intensity that is greater than if we met him face to face, in full daylight. Bereavements are another instance in which great sadness may change rapidly to hilarity. And it is not uncommon to observe that a person who is aroused emotionally may fluctuate among violent manifestations of exuberance, anger, and anxiety.

Thus it may be necessary for an individual to "learn" the emotion of anger by attending to visceral stimuli and relating them to perception and cognitive events. But after one or more exposures, such stimuli are not necessary for subsequent manifestation of emotional behavior in similar situations. The visually perceived stimulus has become a conditioned stimulus, capable of evoking the emotional response.

ANGER AND THE FRUSTRATION-AGGRESSION HYPOTHESIS

Perhaps it would serve a useful purpose if we examined once more traditional and popular notions of frustration, anger, and aggression—this time, with special emphasis upon the emotion of anger. There exists a plausible temptation to think of anger as arising from "frustration," and, in turn, building up "pressure" that must find "release," usually through aggression. Let us take a single case, with the author as the subject under study.

The subject, a fairly educated individual of (presumably) higher than average intelligence, and moreover, a putative authority on human motivation, has a tendency to become manifestly annoyed when, while he is driving, another driver maneuvers his car in what the subject judges to be an incompetent or dangerous manner. Since we are at a moment of unrestrained self-revelation, let it be admitted that our learned, and usually quite tolerant subject, has been known to indulge in language that is anything but complimentary to the other driver. Not only may the latter's mental abilities be questioned, but occasionally the subject may express a strong recommendation that the other's driving privileges be withdrawn. There may even be a daydream of Eternal Justice intervening and inflicting a minor mishap upon the offender.

It is easy to restate the situation here described in terms of "frustration," "anger" (conceptualized as a building up of a tangible quid seeking release), and more or less overt aggression, especially when our subject is observed storming at one of his hapless and quite inoffensive passengers. But the invariances implied by such an interpretation require careful examination. Behaviors like the one described on the part of another driver should have invariant frustrating effects upon the subject. Yet if the other driver happens to belong to the female sex, conforms to broad requirements as to age and proportions, and displays long, ashblond tresses undulating in the air-currents produced by the daring acrobatics performed by her convertible under her nonchalant, although expert guidance, our subject might conceivably experience an inner state somewhat different from "frustration." To vary the picture a little, let us assume that, seeing the other driver only indistinctly, our subject experiences "frustration" over being delayed or endangered. When he recognizes the other's salient qualities, regardless of whether he has already become angry or not, his mood now changes rapidly: he rehearses now—alas, only to himself—suave urbanity and sophisticated wit instead of the punitive measures contemplated only a moment ago. His anger has left him suddenly, without having found any detectable outlet.

Other variations of the theme can be constructed: our subject's anger remains unaltered by perceived changes of the other's attributes, but he shortly has forgotten all about it; or, he realizes that it was he, and not the other, who drove carelessly. Again, we should predict that although the only part of the situation that can be operationally defined as "frustration"—namely the threat of delay produced by the presence of the other vehicle—remained constant, our driver would give evidence of quite different inner states. When we feel justified in describing him as "angry," we have difficulty in separating that inner state, not only in terms of relevant observations, but even conceptually, from the one we conceive as "frustration." Finally, we can find no fluid or gas that corresponds to "anger," and hence must be vented. Sometimes anger results in aggression, sometimes it does not; and in the latter case we can measure no residue of pressure which would evidence that the pernicious substance is still there.

If we were to represent the presumed relationships graphically, they might appear as shown below:

$$
\begin{array}{ccccc}
? & ? & ? & \text{Preparation} & \\
& & & \text{for} & \\
\text{Stimulus} \rightarrow & \text{Frustration} \rightarrow & \text{Anger} \rightarrow & \text{Aggression} \rightarrow & \text{Aggression} \\
\text{(External)} & \text{(Internal)} & \text{(Internal)} & \text{(Internal)} & \text{(External)}
\end{array}
$$

It is the basic point of our lengthy argument that the arrows, which should indicate a lawful relationship, apply only occasionally, and that the three separate inner states here represented are inadequately conceptualized and therefore incapable of separate assessment. The difficulty remains essentially unchanged if we move "frustration" outside the organism, that is, incorporate it in the stimulus. We should, again, be compelled to admit that invariant stimuli produce different states and that the relationship between these states and behaviors are so loosely stated as to allow for little if any prediction.

Therefore, it makes no sense to speak of "anger" as an invariant outcome of certain perceptual events, as might be argued in the case of some animals in whom "anger" (which we now know to be an integral part of an attack response) seems to be elicited invariably by the perception of certain stimuli. Also, anger does not necessarily lead to aggression, nor is aggression always accompanied by anger.

The notion of the scapegoat—which is often adduced to account for anti-Semitism and other forms of prejudice—has often been interpreted in terms of traditional notions of "displacement" of anger (Bettelheim & Janowitz, 1950). Yet when a person, or a group, is made the object of discrimination or persecution, this happens most of the time without any anger on the part of the persecutors. In fact, people who habitually express prejudice or hostility may do so quite without measurable emotional states. We shall see later that prejudice, hate, and hostility are more usefully conceptualized as behavioral habits, which are learned over time and are relatively independent of visceral states.

THE MANY MEANINGS OF ANGER

Finally, and most important, we can carry our examination of anger considerably further and discover that anger has important and complex cognitive correlates, so that it may not be a unitary phenomenon at all. In fact, some of the different emotional behaviors to which the term "anger" is customarily assigned might be among the following:

1. We have already seen that anger is the name given, rather inappropriately, to that portion of the attack-sequence which we observe as occurring, in a stereotyped fashion, in many animals.

2. We sometimes speak of anger to refer to a diffuse and maladaptive agitation displayed by a lower organism and by very young or poorly organized humans upon being presented with a difficult or unsolvable situation. This "anger" response involves very little cognitive evaluation; and even though it sometimes appears to lead to attack, it may well be that this attack is really a random component of the generally agitated behavior.

3. Anger may be classically conditioned. Let us suppose that emotional arousal is associated, through repeated presentation, with certain stimulus situations. When the stimulus situation recurs, so does the arousal. However, because the stimulus situation is also subject to cognitive evaluation ("this is something to be afraid of," or, "this is something to be happy about"), it is not surprising that the emotional state accompanying it is given corresponding labels.

4. It may well be that an emotional response—for example, anger—may be classically conditioned to or associated with certain instrumental preparatory responses that may initially have been selected independently of the emotional state. Thus, a person preparing to engage in an athletic contest, and in some way experiencing visceral changes, may find that such arousal helps him to compete more effectively. The visceral arousal may thus become conditioned to the preparatory behavior through contiguity. Eventually, this emotional response may acquire instrumental value. Recent findings by Shapiro, Crider, and Tursky (1964) suggest that an initially classical response tends to drop out of the organism's response-repertoire, unless its presence over time fulfills an instrumental role. In other words, if the organism "needs" this arousal state in order to perform effectively, the response will endure; if the organism is able to perform without it, it will drop out.

5. As a variant of the above, it is also possible that a person is *fully aware* that being angry helps him to perform, compete, or aggress effectively; he therefore "whips himself into a rage" or makes himself deliberately angry so that he can emit his responses with greater vigor and effectiveness. There is recent evidence (Brehm, Back, & Bogdonoff, 1964; Zimbardo, 1966) that physiological states are to some extent susceptible to cognitive control.

We might also classify under the heading of "anger" the phenomenon of moral or righteous indignation (Stratton, 1923). Here, the adjective "angry," though it denotes a subjective state, defines a situation in which a person marshals his emotional responses against an outrage or injustice believed to be objectively wrong. Stratton discusses other variants of "functional," or deliberately fostered, arousal states, such as "anger" or "rage," in the service of certain religious and nationalistic creeds, aimed at unifying the in-group, and energizing aggressive acts against the out-groups.

6. Finally—and this is a rarely considered possibility—the emotion of anger may actually follow rather than precede the violent act, or increase after it. Let us assume that a person has committed aggression and now feels guilty about it. By saying—and believing—that he was very angry at the time, and perhaps by again producing in himself symptoms of anger and upset, he is thereby able to excuse or justify his behavior to some degree.

It appears, therefore, that the acknowledgement of emotion or anger as a determinant of aggression helps us in the understanding and control of aggressive behavior less than we might initially have thought possible. The basic question has been encumbered by another term; but we still do not have insight into the relationships among antecedent events, inner states, and behaviors.[5]

---

[5] In some respects, Berkowitz's recent theory (1962), which is a modification of the Frustration-Aggression hypothesis, runs parallel to Schachter and Singer's (1962) formulation. It admits that aggression cannot be produced by physiological arousal alone, nor by the sole presentation of a stimulus. Aggression largely occurs because a stimulus has the appropriate aggression-evoking characteristics and because an internal arousal state is present. Now, as we have said many times, it is of course true that there are strong relationships between arousal and aggressive behavior. Berkowitz himself cites evidence of physiological arousal without aggression. Conversely, not only men but even mice (Scott, 1958) have been shown to commit aggression without the concomitant physiological changes, provided that such aggression had become habitually successful. It would appear, therefore, that a retention of even a modified Frustration-Aggression hypothesis has little predictive value.

V

The Acquisition
of Social Behaviors

This chapter presents an overview of learning theories and their applications to social behaviors: classical and instrumental conditioning.

Imitation learning and the role of language in social learning are discussed.

Inferences are drawn regarding unobserved, putative responses by the model, and lead to identification. Learning from several or composite models produces social norms and rules—a conscience is formed! Language as an instrument of complex cognitive processes, and its relevance for complex social behavior. Social motives and values.

WE HAVE NOW EXAMINED some of the problems that arise when aggression among human beings in a social context is discussed, and it has been argued that "classical" formulations that postulate a basic drive, urge, or instinct to aggress are of little value in our quest for the prediction, control, and (it is hoped) the ultimate prevention of aggressive behavior. Perhaps it would not be amiss to point out once more that the argument of this book is not that there does *not* exist, at least among some species, some kind of basic primitive "instinct" toward injuring a fellow member of the species. Indeed, many of the recent animal studies appear to indicate that an aggression pattern—or, preferably, an attack pattern—in mammals can reliably be evoked by appropriate stimulation of certain areas of the brainstem (Glickman & Schiff, 1967). It is also not crucial to our argument to maintain that frustration and aggression are unrelated in practice. Obviously they are not. Instead, the question reduces itself to more basic ones: (1) To what extent do these formulations make our explanation and prediction of human behavior more accurate than no theory-based prediction? (2) Is the gain—if there is a gain—in explanatory and predictive accuracy large enough to matter? Finally (3), is it possible that greater precision can be attained within a different theoretical framework?

It is the inadequacy of existing formulations which prompts the search for new ones. In the present instance, such inadequacy is all too evident. Questions 1 and 2 have already been answered in the negative. It may not be hard to see why "aggression" has come to assume a unique place in the study of man; but in allowing this to happen inquirers may have begged a crucial question, and permitted themselves to be hamstrung by preconceptions. Let us see, therefore, whether question 3 leads to a productive answer.

The sheer number and subtlety of attitudes and response tendencies acquired by a child in the earliest period of his life have an enormous impact upon the development of his entire personality. These individual experiences, which we can quite properly call "learning," pervade every conceivable aspect of his life. Within biological and maturational limits, of course, they affect his behavioral individuality far more than alleged built-in, relatively unchangeable tendencies (instincts), or equally unalterable bonds between specific stimuli and responses (such as frustration—aggression). It is for this reason that the average American-born youth, of, say, Italian descent has a greater resemblance to other American adolescents in terms of his beliefs and habits than to his father, who was raised in the "old country." Or, consider, how even eating habits, although originating from such a basic drive as "hunger," are affected by the person's daily experiences as he grows up; these, obviously, differ not only across ethnic cultures but even within otherwise fairly homogeneous subcultures. In addition, his going to a restaurant at a given time and his ordering certain dishes may depend also only in small part upon the strength of his hunger drive; to a greater degree both acts will depend on his immediate social environment—such as his friends, and their plans for lunch or dinner.

Given this basic, almost trivial, fact, is it not reasonable to speculate that it might be heuristically fruitful to view aggression as one subset or fraction of behaviors, determined in turn by learned attitudes and expectations?

Now, if a case is to be made for social learning as the major factor in aggressive behavior (as well as the altruistic acts to be discussed later), we must first examine the mechanisms of social learning, and then determine whether they are applicable to aggression. The remainder of this chapter deals with the first part of this issue; the next chapter will present a detailed examination of aggression as a socially learned and reinforced class of behaviors.

One of the major controversies in learning deals with the sufficiency or insufficiency of basic conditioning processes to account for all forms of human learning (Skinner, 1953, 1957; Miller & Dollard, 1941; Mowrer, 1950, 1960a, 1960b; Bandura, 1965; Chomsky, 1959). But in any event, the enormous importance of these basic processes is not denied by either faction.[1]

BASIC LEARNING PROCESSES

The simplest process—classical, or Pavlovian, conditioning—consists of the pairing of a stimulus (the "unconditioned" stimulus) that evokes a "natural" response (the "unconditioned," or "unconditional," response) with a previously neutral stimulus. After a few such parings (under certain quite narrow temporal conditions), the previously neutral stimulus will evoke a response (the conditioned response) very similar to that evoked by the natural stimulus: it has become a conditioned stimulus. Pavlov demonstrated this phenomenon with several stimuli. His most famous experiments involved dogs as subjects, with meat powder as the unconditioned stimulus evoking salivation, and a tone as the conditioned stimulus.

Watson and Rayner (1920) subsequently established that the process works also with humans and, more importantly, that the conditioned response need not be limited to such a simple physiological event as salivation. His unfortunate subject, little Albert B., learned to become afraid of a white rat (contrary to a popular belief, held chiefly by the gentler sex, fear of rats is not inborn) after the appearance of the rat had been made to coincide several times with a loud, naturally frightening tone from a steel bar.

It is only a small and quite logical step to infer that almost any event can, through classical conditioning, become a positive- or negative-conditioned stimulus. Just as little Albert learned to fear the white rat because it had been associated with a naturally fearsome event, so can an organism learn to fear or love a person, a group, or anything else of a social nature if there has been previous pairing with unconditioned or "naturally" frightening stimuli, such as pain or a very loud noise, or pleasant ones, such as food, water, or bodily warmth.

The other basic process, called "instrumental conditioning," is somewhat more complex in that it involves skeletal movements, which at another point in history would have been called "voluntary." Here, the organism learns to choose one out of two or more possible responses by being reinforced for the correct one. A rat learning to turn right in a T-shaped maze is a simple instance. Also—and this is very

[1] For a thorough examination of the major current learning theories, see Hilgard and Bower (1966).

important—previously neutral events or objects acquire reinforcing properties by being closely associated in time with such "natural," or "primary,
reinforcers" as food, which is reinforcing when administered (positive
reinforcer), or pain, whose *removal* is a primary reinforcement and which
is, therefore, called a "negative reinforcer." Reinforcers that are not primary are called "secondary reinforcers" or, more generally (because a
secondary reinforcer can, in turn, confer reinforcing properties upon another, hitherto neutral, stimulus), "higher order reinforcers."

Again, there exists considerable controversy over whether such
behavior is elicited in a reflexlike fashion by the environmental configuration acting as a stimulus, as was assumed by Hull (1943), or whether the
stimulus situation serves as a "signal" for the organism to respond. The
proponent of the latter position, Skinner (1953), argues that the organism
"operates" upon his environment when certain conditions (discriminant
stimuli) are present. He therefore calls this type of learning "operant
conditioning." The evidence seems to favor Skinner's position; but both
positions allow these simple responses to form a chain of responses, where-
in each minute response of the organism produces changes in the environmental situation, as well as proprioceptive feedback, which serve as stimuli
for the next response and as a reinforcement for the preceding one.[2]

This chaining of responses accounts for a rat running a maze requiring several turns, a dog picking up a newspaper in its mouth and extending
it to its master, and, traditional behaviorists would maintain, any complete,
goal-directed act by a human. For Skinner, the property of previously
neutral events to acquire reinforcing qualities is not only convenient but
indispensable for the formation of a behavioral chain. A dog that is given
a primary reinforcer after every fractional response, even after it has
been learned, would experience a lengthy interruption while it eats. On
the other hand, the secondary reinforcement given by its own proprioceptive system as well as the environment (translatable as "Oh good, I have
come this far, now the next thing I have to do is . . .") serves to maintain
the ongoing behavioral sequence.[3]

[2] Learning theorists rarely miss an opportunity for controversy. The Hullian
position is that the chain of learning builds from the goal backwards to the starting
point, whereas Skinner has devised elaborate (and convincing) procedures based
upon a learning process that moves forward in time.
[3] A further controversy revolves around the number of basic learning processes.
One position maintains that both classical and instrumental conditioning are
theoretically equivalent (Guthrie, 1940) and that both take place by association
alone, i.e., that no (reinforcing) drive reduction is required. Hull himself viewed
both classical and instrumental conditioning as requiring reinforcement. Another
position views classical conditioning as association learning, and instrumental
learning as contingent upon drive reduction (Mowrer, 1950). To complete the
picture, Spence (1958) holds the opposite position: that classical conditioning
depends upon drive reduction, whereas instrumental conditioning requires only
temporal contiguity or association. Given the recondite nature of drive and drive
reduction, the controversy may continue for some time.

Whatever the outcomes of the controversies will be, some of which have been barely indicated here (it is a fair assumption that some of them will be placed into the archives of obsolescence), it is clear that man, from a very tender age, learns to function in very different types of environment, and to interact with his fellowman in a complex and sophisticated fashion.

In this process, social events can become stimuli that evoke certain behaviors, whether we see them as "eliciting," or as "signals" or "discriminant" stimuli. Not surprisingly, social events can also be reinforcers. Rheingold, Gewirtz, and Ross (1959) have shown that social reinforcers, such as a smile, become effective at an early age, and are apparently primary in that they need not be paired with proven drive reducers to establish their effectiveness (as is the case, for instance, in the training of a dog, who must learn that the word "No" has negative connotations by repeated, concurrent slaps and vocalizations). But because the contiguity of any neutral event with a pleasant or unpleasant one confers to that neutral event similar connotations of pleasantness or unpleasantness, thereby turning it into secondary reinforcers, it is easy to see how social events, such as words of praise, can become reinforcing, not only to maintain a behavioral sequence, but also as ultimate reward. That social reinforcers are effective with adults is also shown, among others, by the studies of Verplanck (1955) and Greenspoon (1955), which affected the type and frequency of specific types of verbal behaviors made by their subjects by verbal approval (Verplanck, 1955), and even a simple sound of approval, such as *mmm-hum* (Greenspoon, 1955).

Let it be noted, in passing, that a response to words does not in every case imply symbolic processes. The sound, and even the visual configuration of a printed word, can serve as a stimulus or signal even to an animal. The dog responding to his name, or reprimanded by his master with the words "bad dog," responds to these stimuli very much as he would to nonverbal stimuli, because the sound of the words has become a conditional aversive stimulus through repeated pairings with unconditioned aversive events.

WORDS AND MEANINGS IN SOCIAL LEARNING

Humans, however, soon learn to use words in a more complex fashion. A child called by his name responds to a stimulus that could very well have been a whistle with a certain pitch. To him, his name is a symbol for a complex entity, himself, which can enter into a great number of relationships with his environment. Skinner (1957) has made a strong case to the effect that all behavior, even human verbal behavior, can be reduced to the instrumental paradigm. His argument has been questioned on logical grounds by Chomsky (1959). But for our purposes another, more immediate criticism comes to mind: not only people but even rats can learn to imitate or match the choices of a model (Miller & Dollard, 1941).

MODEL AND IMITATION LEARNING

In observing imitation of a model, we can readily distinguish between the copying of specific movements, or molecular behavior, and a more integrated, molar imitation, such as a rat moving toward the same goal as the model, but not necessarily copying its gait, its speed, or its sniffing at various points. In such a situation a rat would be reinforced, not for copying a specific response, but rather for copying a complex behavior sequence of another rat.

It is possible to regard imitation itself as a class of behaviors learned through reinforcement (Miller & Dollard, 1941). But such a theory still presupposes that tangible rewards accrue to the imitator and, given the relative inefficiency of latent learning, it implies that in order to be "learned," such imitation must occur soon after observation of the model (Bandura & Walters, 1963). However, everyday observation shows that much imitation learning occurs without immediate performance by the learner, and therefore necessarily occurs without reward. Often, it is only much later that this behavior appears, and an amazed and sometimes embarrassed parent may discover that his child is reproducing verbal or other behavior that previously the child had given no evidence of even having noticed. Bandura and Walters (1963) and Bandura (1965) therefore distinguish between the *acquisition* of a behavioral repertoire (and, it might be argued by extension, one of attitudes and emotions) and its *performance* or *manifestation*. The acquisition of behaviors occurs most frequently through imitation, while it is the reinforcement contingencies, or expectations of rewards and punishments, that determine their occurrence.

In taking this two-factor model as our point of departure, it should be stressed once more that other processes of acquisition are not denied. Also, the assertion, above, regarding reinforcement contingencies in no sense implies that some kind of physiological drive must have been reduced. Reinforcement, positive or negative, may be taken to include sophisticated environmental events—and even symbolically mediated, self-produced ones (such as a person's telling himself that he has "acted nobly").

THE LEARNING OF NORMS

If we were to draw inferences from these studies and common observation, we might hypothesize that the child adopts a response imitating the parent, which earns him approval from the parent. If Dad rewards Sonny for acting like him, and shows cold indifference when Sonny imitates his vociferous Uncle Joe, it follows that the boy is likely to emit the approved behaviors. He will be "just like Dad," at least as long as hi father's approval has positive reinforcement value. Later, he is able to visualize or imagine this approval, and to administer praise to himself He has "internalized" rules, or has formed a "conscience."

The theory is not impaired by what appears, at first sight, to be a serious limitation: that neither the stimulus situation nor the behavio emitted are ever exact replicas of the situation in which the model wa observed. One needs only the additional and familiar concepts of (stimulu and response) generalization and discrimination (with their admittedl complex implications regarding the *dimensions* along which these processe can occur) in order to account for a variety of situations leading to on of a class of "related" responses when one of a class of "related" stimulus situations occurs.

An even more complex form of using others as models for one' behavior consists of an identification process. Here, the model is seer as either very desirable, or awesome (Freud, 1914; A. Freud, 1946) Not only does the identifier imitate observed behaviors, but he also adopt the model's attitudes and beliefs. Thus, when faced with a nev situation—that is, one in which the model was never observed—the belief and attitudes adopted by the identifier allow him to infer (not necessaril correctly) how the model would have acted had he been in the preser situation, and to act accordingly. Such an identifier might say to himself "I am sure Dad would have stood up to that bully; therefore, I am goin to do so, too."

BECOMING A PART OF SOCIETY

The acquisition of other people's values and beliefs need not b limited to examples by a single model. Mead (1934) speaks of "a genera ized other," a composite abstraction which serves as a transmitter of th norms of a given culture. This form of social identification—or in Riesmar Glazer, and Denney's (1950) term, "other-directedness"—would becom operative through a person's asking himself: "Now, what am I expecte (by my neighbors, professional colleagues, etc.) to feel and to do in th situation?" and following their imagined guidance.

Even a conforming or other-directed person need not be conceive as devoid of other motives that may interfere with total and unquestionin conformity. Our argument assumes only that symbolically mediated gene alizations of this kind can extend social learning beyond the simple imit tion of observed behaviors of individual models. We might also mentio that Riesman's "inner-directed" man—that is, the person who acts i accordance with his conscience rather than follows the actual or inferre dictates of others—operates on a higher plane, both ethically and cogn tively. The mediational processes whereby an "ideal self" or a perfer

eneralized other" replaces some specific arbiter require at least the addi-
onal step of inferring a behavioral code for this ideal, nonexistent person
the basis of observing existing others, and integrating and reconciling
eir beliefs and actions into consistent generalizations.

The socialized individual must have learned a great deal more than
aique responses to specific stimulus situations. Even in the very simplest
' societies, he must have an enormous repertoire of laws, norms, and
les, many of which may apply to events he may never experience. He
s some idea, though possibly inaccurate, about laws concerning murder
d the inheritance of land, neither of which may be likely to be relevant
his life. He is in a position to offer at least an opinion on group
lidarity among front line soldiers, although he has been, and will remain,
civilian all his life.

More important, our citizen must know what complex set of be-
viors his society expects of him in his capacities of, say, a bank clerk,
husband, a father, a member of a lodge, and a neighbor. In his inter-
tions with others, a person learns what is expected of him—and what
may expect of others—in regard to social positions. He learns what
haviors are expected of him in his roles of, say, college student, son,
d boyfriend, as well as in the much less formally defined roles of "life
the party" or "classroom cut-up." Sarbin and Allen (1968) view the
mplex and many-faceted performances of an individual in his society
terms of role theory. Proper enactment of a role requires (a) accurate
rception of what the role entails, and (b) the skills necessary to perform
accordance with these expectations. Role-learning is thus the learning
a general pattern of attitudes and behaviors such as those of an abstrac-
d other person similar to oneself. We learn something about how we
ight to behave as, say, a boy of twelve, a college freshman, a jobholder,
husband, a voter, and on and on.

This social learning has various aspects. First of all, we have to
arn what are the norms or expectations associated with a given role.
or a boy of twelve there are certain attitudinal and behavioral expecta-
ons, such as "don't be afraid of the dentist," "think about college,"
e polite to adults." Notice, however, how all these expectations reflect
e viewpoint of some quite specific other person, presumably the boy's
ther or guardian. It is not hard to see that, for example, the boy's
er group might have a different set of expectations, which are either
dditional to the paternal ones, or may even conflict with them.

NGUAGE AND COMPLEX COGNITIVE PROCESSES IN
   SOCIALIZATION

These processes of identification or role-taking appear to involve
e type of symbolic mediation which would be impossible without lan-
age (Langer, 1948). One no longer needs to perceive a physical stim-

ulus situation in order to execute a response. A symbolic equivalent, su<
as the printed or spoken word "apple," can take the place of the origin
object. Similarly, the person "identifying" with another or others, assimila
ing laws and norms, and cherishing many forms of approval by his fello<
man, could not do so without understanding and using language at a lev
that differs qualitatively from that of words as signs or signals.

The role of language in socialization is not limited to that of mec
ating symbolic processes. It is also the fundamental tool for another, e
tremely efficient class of learning processes which are, once again, "socia<
by definition—namely the transmission by one person to another of dire
instructions, such as "Do that"; of contingency instructions, such as "
x occurs, do y"; or of contingency information, which takes the for
"If you do x, then y will happen." (Since we are mainly concerned wi
behavioral consequences of learning, we are only peripherally intereste
in the transmission of information that is irrelevant to a person's behavic
although one might argue that no item of knowledge is ever irrelevant
Obviously, the transmission of information and instruction by means <
language can be considered a social process even where the reading <
a document is concerned. Somebody had to write the book of instruction
or draw the map.

SOCIAL MOTIVES AND VALUES

Social motives such as ambition, loyalty, conscientiousness, and p
triotism can be seen also as developing through social learning. Thu
ambition may develop because a child has repeatedly been rewarde
not for accomplishing a given task, but rather for "having done
good job," or, "having done one's best." (It is not maintained th
ambition may not arise in other ways, such as a means of defeating <
showing up a disliked person.) This early reinforcement, and such pr
cesses as comparisons of present situations with past ones, can then le<
to a lifetime of dedicated endeavor.

The learning of values may proceed by yet another process. T<
child engages in certain behaviors, accidentally, imitatively, or becau<
they have been reinforced occasionally. If he does so successfully f<
a number of times, we should expect that attitudes may develop whic
are congruent with that behavior. Ostensibly, the process hypothesize
here differs from those of dissonance reduction (Festinger, 1957) ar
self-persuasion (Bem, 1967). These deal with behaviors undertaken und<
minimal coercion, or with adverse consequences for which the actor mu
then find a "justification." A highly successful behavior, on the oth<
hand, is precisely the kind that needs *no* such justification, because <
can be seen to have been undertaken for reward alone. A successful <
rewarded behavior may result in subtle social reinforcements even whe

here *is* a tangible reward present, particularly if the situation recurs re-
eatedly. Thus, a person who has bullied another once, and has gotten
way with it, presumably requires no justification for his successful act.
f, however, the act of bullying, thus reinforced, is perpetrated a number
f times, and with considerable success, more than just a specific habit
s acquired. The person may become more and more convinced that "life
s a jungle, and you have to look out for Number One. It works, doesn't
?" Or he may even perceive covert social approval, translatable as "Well,
' it were wrong, I wouldn't be getting away with it so often, would I?
t must be all right, then, to push the other guy around a bit when he
as something I want."

Thus, a value may develop through self-observation and induction,
ndependently from values transmitted directly, or "internalized" through
ffective affinity with others. These values, once formed, have of course
quite similar effect upon subsequent behaviors as values acquired by
ther means.

In examining the entire argument for social learning, one is struck
ot by the need to support the evidence for the existence of social stimuli
nd reinforcers, but by their pervasiveness. Quite clearly, social stimuli
nd reinforcers play an enormous part in human behavior, from the earliest
tages of infancy. Social learning takes place at all levels of
omplexity—from simple classical conditioning of social stimuli to com-
lex mediation of social motives. We shall now see how the theory is
elevant to aggressive behavior.

VI

Social Learning and Aggression

Learning theories and their applicability to the study of aggression are discussed. Aggression has 3 components: aggressor, victim, and situation. How is the desirability (or otherwise) of aggression learned by the developing child? Parents are both models and dispensers of reinforcements, and in these two capacities may induce conflicting motives in the child. Parental permissiveness toward aggression plays an important role in the formation of the child's social behaviors. Aggressive models also influence children in the acquisition of aggressive habits and behaviors. Are there any unlearned stimuli for aggression? Learning to be a victim or target of aggression: How a (blameless) prospective victim can contribute toward eliciting aggression against himself. A look at the enormous importance of cultural norms and (momentary) situational determinants of aggression. The phenomenon of "contagion" in crowds and in groups may result in aggression. Committing aggression "obediently." Mass media may play a unique role as transmitters of aggressive norms.

W E ARE NOW FACED with the task of examining the adequacy of th social learning theory outlined in the previous chapter as it applies t the specific topic with which we are concerned. Specifically, we must stud the evidence in order to determine whether this theory will allow us t predict the occurrence and intensity of aggressive behavior with greate exactness than it would be possible for us to do with the previously dis cussed models. Let us remember that we are concerned with what the statis tician would call "discovering the major source of variance"; in othe words, we must find the major determinants of aggressive behaviors fc specific individuals, and in specific situations.

It is of considerable importance to examine various aspects of the aggressor: his previous experiences in terms of his personal background, the way he perceives a given situation, and his experiences with the present target, and also with people in some way resembling that target. As we know, some people develop generic aggressiveness to a much more intense degree than others. They develop, as it were, a *habit* to aggress. But it takes (at least) two to make an aggressive situation; hence, there may be considerable value in looking at both the aggressor and the target, as well as at explicit and implicit cultural values, *and* at the specific situation in which the aggression occurs.

The target, or stimulus, has been shown to be of considerable importance in the elicitation of aggressive behavior. We know from everyday experience that some people just seem to be asking to be punched in the nose, whereas others elicit meekness from even the most notorious bully. There are, in other words, likely and unlikely targets for aggression. It is also true that some stimulus persons may elicit aggression from one individual but not from another.

In addition to inividual experiences affecting aggressive tendencies, the individual also acquires, as part of the socialization process, a set of cultural norms regarding the appropriateness of aggressiveness. These norms are partly general, partly situation-specific. We learn to differentiate readily among situations that favor aggressiveness, such as wars, battles, and even competitive body contact sports, and those that do not favor such behaviors, such as discussion groups and university seminars (though at the time of this writing, some modification of the last statement seems called for).

Thus our approach to the study of aggressive behavior in interpersonal relations (and as I have stated before, it is really in this context only that it makes sense to speak of "aggression") will be to study the characteristics of the aggressor, the properties of the stimulus person who elicits the aggressive response, and finally, and perhaps most importantly, the general cultural norms and specific attributes of the situation in which the aggression occurs. This approach is based upon the surmise that aggression cannot be studied as a single, unitary phenomenon, and that the events which lead to the ultimate event, characterized as "aggression," may differ very widely in terms of the individuals involved, the social context in which the act occurs, and the meaning the act has for the participants and for observers. Once we have overcome the ingrained preconception of aggression as a unique attribute of people and animals, it becomes overwhelmingly clear that processes whereby we learn other social behaviors must be operative also in the learning of aggressive tendencies.

In the remainder of this chapter we shall examine the occurrence of aggression as it is affected by characteristics of the aggressor, the victim,

LIBRARY ST. MARY'S COLLEGE

cultural values, and the immediate circumstances of the aggressive situation, and attempt to understand the findings in terms of social learning, as proposed in the preceding chapter. The final section of this chapter deals with an aspect of cultural transmission of norms which may be especially effective, and therefore crucial, that is the function of mass media.

THE AGGRESSOR

Almost everyone had been an aggressor at some time or another—that is, he has engaged in an act against another person, with reasonable expectations that it might result in some injury or damage to the other. However, it is certainly appropriate to distinguish between people who aggress frequently, and upon slight provocation, and others who do so only rarely. This observation considered by itself is not surprising, since it constitutes just another individual difference. Our purpose, however, is not simply to *observe* these differences, and ascribe them to some mythical agent or force. Instead, we shall look at observable and definable antecedents in a person's experience which might conceivably produce tendencies to more or less frequent aggression.

(The classification of individuals in terms of their "aggressiveness" can proceed by several criteria. "Self-report" may not be as misleading a technique as it is often believed to be, especially when it is made clear to the person reporting about himself that no opprobrium attaches to the various attributes he may ascribe to himself. However, ratings by others, concealed observation during time samples, and various paper and pencil measures have found greater acceptance, even though their validity in predicting aggressiveness over a variety of situations is by no means impressive.)

The Transmission of Norms and Values

The individuals who are instrumental in our socialization—that is, who contribute toward our becoming more or less law-abiding and normative members of society—also transmit to us those attitudes and tendencies that relate to aggressive behavior. This is not to say that a child will become either an exact replica of his parents, or a behavioral compendium of parental teaching. Children often fail to live up to their parents' instructions, and equally often do not imitate or copy their observed behaviors and inferred attitudes. Nevertheless, the role of the parents as socializing agents is a powerful one, and has been recognized since the earliest records of human civilization. Upon the parent rests the heavy responsibility to inculcate in the child those values, beliefs, attitudes, and behavior tendencies that will make him a useful member of his society. The occasional unfitness of certain parents to be such instruments of a society's value system, and the occasional failure of fit and well-intentioned parents to accomplish this task does not negate the fundamental role they play in most societies. Even in utopian societies, in which the task of socialization is not entrusted to parents, it is fully understood that the child must learn from the adult members of the society. This necessity is accepted even by the most ardent proponents of innateness theories. Very few people today would recommend that the child be allowed to develop entirely on his own—without the guidance of his society. (Although there is an anecdote, presumably apocryphal, that, in the thirteenth century, Emperor Frederick II believed that Hebrew was the language a child would naturally acquire if this process were not impeded by the linguistic teachings of those around him. In order to test his theory he collected a few orphaned infants and placed them in isolation. It is reported that they all perished before the imperial theory could be adequately tested.)

Aggressive and Nonaggressive Parents

There is no sound basis for believing that if we were to find that aggressive parents are more likely to have aggressive children than nonaggressive parents, a hereditary transmission of "aggressive" genes has taken place. We should be more inclined to conclude that aggressive parents either set their children aggressive examples—that is, they are aggressive models for their children—or they are more rewarding toward their children when the latter indulge in aggressive behaviors. A father who derogates other people in violent terms, who graphically describes the injuries he might inflict upon them, who perhaps even attacks them physically, acts not only as a model for social interaction, but often encourages his son to "stand up for yourself," presumably also reviling him for any sign of "cowardice" exemplified by avoiding a fight.

A somewhat conflicting prediction would result for aggressive parents if it were hypothesized that (a) they do act (inevitably) as aggressive models for their children, and (b) they are more punitive than nonaggressive parents, and therefore might tend to punish *any* kind of undesirable behavior, including aggressive behavior, more rigorously than less aggressive parents. A child might learn, then, that it is desirable to aggress against people other than his father; but the negative emotional response conditioned to any aggressive situation might become strong enough to eliminate all aggressive behavior.

The relationship between parental (especially paternal) and filial aggressiveness becomes even more confused when we consider that children can learn aggressiveness from many sources, not merely from their parents, and that it is largely the *permissiveness* of parents toward such aggressive behavior which allows it to endure. On the other hand, the inflexibility or severity of the parents might also, indirectly, lead to aggression in the child. It is likely that children who are denied their desires more frequently, that is, who become frustrated, might seek gratification in different ways. Without resorting to the fallacies of the Frustration-Aggression hypothesis (discussed in Chapter III), it is quite valid to predict the likelihood of a positive relationship between frustration and aggression, not because an unalterable bond between them is assumed, but because of the observation that frustrated individuals, being nonquiescent, indulge in alternative behaviors, *some* of which may well be aggressive, and that they are in some instances rewarded by the attainment of a desired object.

A child who is denied permission to attend the movies must find something else to do. Annoying his younger brother may become the selected alternative behavior, not arrived at through a random process, but because the "frustrated" child perceives some likelihood that in this manner he can get back at his parents, or perhaps even blackmail them into greater future cooperation. Frustration, in this instance, would be conceived not as an elicitor of aggression but as a stimulus for engaging in certain behaviors that may have rewarding properties.

It can thus be seen that the interaction between the parents' attitudes and behaviors and those of their children is a complex one, and that no simple relationship can be assumed. Aggressive or violent parents may well induce in their children conflicting tendencies of imitation and of fear. Nonaggressive, but strict, parents may increase the likelihood of aggressive behavior resulting in gratification and thereby acquiring considerable habit strength. Permissive parents, though providing nonaggressive models and reducing the likelihood that a desired but "frustrated" activity might lead to alternative, possibly aggressive, acts, may allow their children to *get away* with undesirable behavior. For instance, Sears, Maccoby, and Levin (1957) presented circumstantial evidence to the effect that either a mother's severity (aggressiveness) *or* her permissiveness toward the child's behavior can engender aggressiveness in the child. However, the findings are less clear than one would hope for. The ratings of the children were made by their teachers, but those of the mothers were based on self-description. The finding with regard to the mothers is subject to even more than the usual criticism because, unfortunately, the impression that a person may seek to convey to even a skilled interviewer may indicate behavior that is quite different from her actual behavior toward her child. Assuming, however, that the finding is reliable, it is indicative chiefly of *methods* whereby aggressiveness can be reduced or avoided, that is, by nonviolent firmness; but it still gives few clues as to which of the above-mentioned processes engender aggressive *tendencies*. Since even nonaggressive mothers had aggressive children, it is possible that those children modeled themselves after other people in preference to their mothers.

Sears, Pintler, and Sears (1946) found that boys whose fathers had left their homes showed less aggression in a play situation than those boys whose fathers were still present. Conversely, girls from father-absent homes showed more aggression than those from father-present homes. It might be hypothesized here that boys model themselves upon their fathers (who show a customary and normative amount of aggressiveness in our society), whereas girls, who model themselves upon their mothers, presumably had had more aggressive mother models where the father had no longer been living with the family. (I shall not engage in any speculation as to the cause-effect relationship between maternal aggressiveness and father-presence in the home; presumably, a reasonable case could be made for more than one hypothesis.) At the same time it was interesting to note that in the instance of father-present families the doll figures toward which the boys displayed aggression were the facsimiles of their fathers. Thus the father seems to have been both a model for aggressive behavior and the recipient of the behaviors thus learned. Interesting relationships were found by Kagan (1958): aggressive boys produced more fantasy stories involving anger between parent and child, whereas nonaggressive boys produced themes of dependency on adults. We must again keep in mind that these projective devices allow only the most speculative inference about the relationship of children's response-tendencies to parental behavior. Allowing for the built-in shortcomings of these studies, however, it may be assumed that aggressive parents act as a model for the child. This interpretation is further corroborated by the finding that nonaggressive boys reported their mother rather than their father as being the major punitive agent. Kagan (1958) interprets this last finding in terms of the nonaggressive boys' anxiety about being rejected by their mother rather than by their father. He suggests that such anxiety should lead to relatively strong inhibitory responses with respect to aggressive behaviors, because mothers customarily are disapproving of aggression. It might also be argued, however, that the mother, although a punitive agent, does not constitute as powerful a model for the boy as the father, and that her punitive, aggressive behaviors are less likely to be assimilated.

Our insistence upon the importance of parents as socializing agents should not be countered by assertions that some parents who disapprove of aggression nevertheless have aggressive children, and vice versa. It is not valid to object that some children who grow up with very little if any parental guidance often seem to develop into especially aggressive and hostile individuals. After all, the process of socialization as we see it involves learning principles discussed in the previous chapter. The commonplace fact that parents during the early years of a child's life are the most frequent administrators of reinforcement (both positive and negative) and punishment, as well as models for the acquisition of behaviors and attitudes, does not deny the frequent opportunity to (a) learn from others and (b) obtain reinforcements from other sources. Even a randomly emitted behavior, reinforced quite by accident, can acquire habit strength. A child, although not taught or instructed to hit another child, may very well do so randomly or accidentally, and by being reinforced for it—again, accidentally (for instance, by the other child's relinquishing a desired toy)—may thus have taken the first step toward acquiring a habit of aggression. It might then take more than parental admonition to undo the effects of such reinforcing events, especially if they occur repeatedly. In studying the acquisition of aggressive habits in the developing person, we must therefore look, first of all, to the "official" socializing agents who reward certain behaviors and punish others (although often not as consistently as could be desired) and who, deliberately or unintentionally, model behaviors and attitudes for the observing child. Having done so, we cannot afford to ignore the frequently fortuitous experiences that provide a child either with rewards for certain behaviors or with an opportunity to observe others being rewarded for undesirable behaviors. It might also be reasonable to assume that adults other than the parents function as powerful objects of identification, or at least imitation, for the child. Here, we do have rather convincing experimental evidence to report.

Experimental Studies of Modeling

A number of studies examining the effects of a model's behavior upon the child's imitation have been conducted by Bandura and Walters and their collaborators. The standard procedure of these authors consists in having an adult punch a large bobo doll, sometimes with accompanying verbal aggression, and observe children's subsequent "aggression" against the doll. In a series of studies, Bandura, Ross, and Ross (1961, 1963a, 1963b) showed that children imitated aggressive models and, more important, also engaged in other forms of aggressive behavior after observing such a model. Also, the observed effects of the model's behavior were important: where the aggressive model was rewarded, children showed more aggressive behavior than where he was punished. Bandura and Walters (1963) make a strong case for the nefarious effects that the antisocial or harmful behaviors of the model might have upon the observing child. From this, we might justifiably infer that it may be desirable to avoid bad company.

It could be maintained that the authors tend to overemphasize some of their findings. For instance, it could be asserted that the imitation of such behavior as punching a bobo doll need not denote a learning of "aggression." The child might simply be impelled to imitate any behavior he observed on the part of the adult, without classifying it cognitively, and therefore without engaging in any generalization. Such generalization effects, however, *were* found by these authors. Some of the children showed great originality in inventing new forms of aggression, which carried over into other play situations. These findings could mean a symbolic generalization of the model's observed behavior, or a simpler inference on the part of the child that the situation is one in which aggressive acts are desirable.

Are There Unconditioned Stimuli for Aggression?

Viewing the aggressor in terms of the learning processes discussed in the preceding chapter, we find that the stimulus situation is rarely one that elicits an aggressive response unconditionally. It may be that some stimuli are capable of evoking a classically conditioned, aversive emotional response. Thus a person may have been conditioned early in life to fear or hate people with certain stimulus characteristics, such as a dark face or a dentist's lab coat. Such a response, however, need not lead to aggression. As we have seen, even the physiological arousal state appears to be amendable to reduction through a cognitive reinterpretation of the stimulus situation (Hokanson & Shetler, 1961).

The Acquisition of Aggressive Propensities

On the other hand, individuals differ strongly in the range of situations and stimuli to which they respond with aggression. The processes whereby these propensities are learned can, as we have seen, occur at every level of complexity. A target may have classically conditioned aversive properties. Sometimes he is attacked because either such behavior has been rewarded in the past more frequently (instrumental conditioning), or the attacker imitates and identifies with a real or composite model. The transmission of *instructions* ("Hit him." Or "If he opens his mouth, let him have it.") or *information* ("If you act like a man, people will respect you.") by means of language may serve, not only to induce the specific behavior, but also to establish social motives that have aggression for their expressed goals, or that embody aggression as a frequent and acceptable means of attaining other ostensible goals.

Finally, even in a situation where a conflict exists—that is, where there is present not only a readiness to aggress, but also an inhibition against it—some individuals may have learned these inhibitions less intensely than others, so that such a conflict impedes aggression only in situations where the motive to commit it is quite weak.

That a cognitive labeling of sorts takes place, and that a person not only acquires specific aggressive response habits but also a frame of mind or structure of personality that favors aggressive behaviors, are indicated by a study by Berkowitz (1960). Individuals scoring high on a hostility scale also displayed greater annoyance toward their partners in a work situation when aroused to anger. Everyday observation, too, indicates that there are some grounds for differentiating habitually hostile individuals from those usually displaying low hostility. This, of course, is not to say that the low hostile individual never aggresses, or that the high hostile individual may not have moments of tenderness. It seems sound, however, to infer a habitual style of interaction with others. An interesting study by Feierabend and Feierabend (1965) indicates that distinctions in degree of aggressiveness can be made even across nations. Again, we would be inclined to ascribe these differences not to genetic ethnic, or racial factors, but rather to different cultural traditions in which children are raised.

Finally, the frequent engaging in aggression appears to have a three-pronged effect: it enhances, in the traditional (Hullian) sense of the word, the habit strength of aggressive behaviors through more frequent successful "trials"; it lowers the threshold for aggression—that is, aggression is triggered more readily, and more situations are seen as calling for aggressive responses; and, finally, the association of previously neutral stimuli with aggressive acts imparts to these stimuli inherent negative qualities. Notably, this can occur through various processes. Events preceding an aggressive act are often unpleasant, and the stimulus thereby acquires classically conditioned, aversive properties. Man, however, also needs to believe in his own righteousness; having attacked, he can justify his actions to himself by ascribing negative properties to the victim by means of mediational processes, or cognitive reassessments commonly known as "rationalization." In the next chapter we shall see how certain classes of stimuli are persistently perceived as having aversive properties, as the result of being seen habitually as objects of attack and derogation.

Social learning theory, then, provides a very useful and, above all, a testable way of explaining, and perhaps predicting, individual differences in resorting to aggressive behaviors. The habits and tendencies of the potential aggressor, however, constitute only one aspect of an aggressive situation.

THE TARGET OF AGGRESSION

Examining now the target of aggressive behavior, we find that it is not difficult to construct a model for the learning of passive, submissive, perhaps even masochistic, tendencies. Learning theory provides us with the processes to account for the behavior of an individual who is frequently rewarded for submitting to aggression, and perhaps even invites aggression. Most of us have met the particularly unfortunate child who seems to elicit attacks from bigger and stronger children. Not only does such a child seem to derive some satisfaction from being continually insulted or beaten up, but he actually acquires a legitimate place in the hierarchical structure of the peer group. He is the "butt" or the scapegoat upon whom others practice their aggressions in a situation that appears to be mutually rewarding in that the aggressor proves his vigor, and the victim gains the attention of someone who otherwise might be too far above him to pay him any heed. It is conceivable that the recent outcry of young Negro militants against "Uncle Tomism" is partly aimed at the alleged tendency of some Negroes who acquire sufferance and perhaps even some degree of status, by submitting to, and inviting, the aggression of white racists.

Although the distinction may be a subtle one, our concern here is with those individuals who become victims of aggression because of roles assigned to them or assumed by them, rather than because of unchanging characteristics of a racial or national nature (a topic to be examined in the next chapter). It is clear that the study of aggressive behavior, with all its sophistication, is still incomplete in this respect. Is aggression—at least some of the time, and to some degree—ascribable, not only to the aggressor and to the situational determinants we shall shortly examine, but also to some characteristic, perhaps even a deliberate act, by the victim?

This may sound like a cynical question. It seems at first sight that to attach blame to the victim for being aggressed against bears all the connotations of the Nazis' common tendency to blame the Jews for being the victims of genocide. The matter, however, may not be as simple as all that. Clearly, the question of whether stimulus aspects of the prospective victim facilitate or encourage aggression must be answered empirically, rather than by a priori assertions. Furthermore, to assert that certain characteristics of an object of aggression facilitate the perpetration of such aggression by someone else is not equivalent to "blaming" the victim for being a victim. Such findings might, instead, lead us toward a better understanding of some of the subtler processes involved in an aggressive interaction.

At a very simple level, it can be easily conceded that a person whom a potential aggressor perceives as "guilty" in some way may elicit aggression for various reasons, such as (a) vengeance: The attacker perceives his aggression as an act of retribution or justice, ordained by the law of talion[1]; (b) recovery: The attacker wishes to recover some tangible object which he believes the victim has deprived him of; (c) deterrence: The aggressor attacks the victim in order to deter him from possible future transgressions (it should always be clear that these "transgressions" as perceived by the attacker may be entirely subjective and need have no correspondence in fact); (d) reform or education: The attacker believes that he is "teaching" the other "a lesson"—that is, he may (in all sincerity) believe that he is contributing to the reform or

---

[1] "An eye for an eye and a tooth for a tooth."

education of the victim by teaching him that the act the victim is supposed to have committed is wrong, and must not be repeated; (e) deterrence of others: The aggressor is "setting an example" by aggressing against the victim. He expects to deter other possible observers from committing transgressions similar to those perceived as having been perpetrated by the victim, and in order to achieve such a goal, he may be quite ready to demand the life of the victim.

However, the stimulus qualities of a victim may operate in far subtler fashion. For instance, Berkowitz and Geen (1966) performed the following study:

Male subjects were either angered or treated in a neutral fashion in an experimental situation by a person who had been introduced either as Kirk or as Bob. They then saw either a prizefight in which the actor *Kirk* Douglas portrayed a rather ruthless boxer, or an equally exciting movie about a track race. Finally, the participants were given a legitimate opportunity to administer electric shocks to the person who had previously angered them (or treated them neutrally). The greatest number of shocks was given by people who had been made angry, had seen the prizefight, and had met the instigator under the name of Kirk. The authors explain their findings by hypothesizing that the identical names of the prizefighter and instigator had produced associations that led to heightened aggression. In a later study by the same authors (1967), similar findings were obtained even when the person who had angered the subjects was introduced by name only *after* the film had been seen. Apparently, then, the sequence in which this association was built up did not matter. In an earlier study, Berkowitz (1965b) found that when the instigator himself was introduced as a boxer, he provoked more aggression than when he had been introduced as a speech major.

Some complex relationships were found by Kaufmann and Marcus (1965) between the similarity which the subject perceived to exist between himself and a fictitious target of aggression. Generally, people were less likely to aggress against others who were seen as "similar" to themselves than against "dissimilar" people; and they were more aggressive if they tended to perceive dissimilarity in important rather than unimportant characteristics, even though the degree of *overall* perceived similarity was unrelated to the amount of expressed aggression. It was also found that the differential aggression against a "dissimilar" rather than a "similar" target—that is, an increased sensitivity to and resentment of dissimilarity—was confined to habitually hostile males who had been angered. For various reasons, then, some people provoke more attacks against themselves than do others.

More generally, it is not difficult to argue that sometimes people provoke attacks from others because they remind them in some way of someone who has angered them (this subjective similarity is only superficially similar to the traditional notions of displacement—the former entails symbolic processes and cognitive evaluation; the latter represents stimulus generalization along a readily definable, physical continuum), or because the person in some way has connotations that make an attack upon him more "legitimate." A boxer, for example, can readily be seen as a "proper target."

We have, then, several ways in which the victim could conceivably contribute through no fault of his own to the aggression perpetrated against him. The victim may be a more "legitimate" target than others because of his profession (or, as a more tragic instance, because of certain religious, racial, or ethnic characteristics, a topic we shall explore further in the next chapter), or because of a striking combination of acts which the victim has committed, or because of associations that the attacker forms between certain characteristics of the victim and aggressive situations that have occurred in other contexts. This would be the case, for instance, if the victim reminded the aggressor of an earlier slight, inflicted by another person; but the "reminder" could also be quite vague, and not involve personal similarities.

It should be pointed out here that the stimulus characteristics of the victim are not synonymous with those commonly associated with discrimination or prejudice. For instance, to argue that a policeman or a boxer is perceived, by most individuals, as a more legitimate target for aggression than is a crippled old lady is not to say that most individuals are (unfavorably) prejudiced against policemen or boxers; the very contrary may be the case. At any rate, this aspect of the aggressive act is one that has been least explored in psychological investigation, and much research needs to be done.

CULTURAL NORMS AND SITUATION DETERMINANTS OF AGGRESSION

The most striking findings in our examination so far of the phenomenon of aggression deal with cultural and situational variables, which exceed by far the individual propensities toward aggression and the possible aggression-eliciting characteristics of a victim. Everyday examples are not hard to find. Even bullies rarely fight in a church or in a funeral parlor, and an entirely meek individual may kill without feeling compunction in the "appropriate" setting, such as a national conflict or a riot. In other words, an aggressive event is more likely to occur in a bar or in a stadium than in a church, or in a living room, even though the same people may be involved. This does not mean that whenever people have the irresistible urge to fight, they leave their living room and repair to a bar or to a football field. The process seems to work quite differently. Individuals may spend many years staying in their living rooms, going to their offices, or making occasional devotional visits, without becoming involved in fights. When, quite haphazardly, they visit a football game or a bar (or, perhaps, a political demonstration), however, the likelihood of their becoming involved in some aggressive act becomes much greater.

It is almost tautological to say that for some places certain behaviors are more suitable than others. To admit this, however, and to concede that the frequence and the intensity of behaviors in certain settings exceed that of such behaviors in other locales is to endow these environmental characteristics with properties that are generally believed to be located within the individual committing an aggressive act.

If one really stops to examine the situational characteristics in which aggression occurs, and then pits these powerful determinants against personality characteristics, it quickly becomes clear that the former play a very substantial, and usually decisive, part in the commission of aggressive acts. Situational and personality determinants, however, are not always easily untangled. In some instances we shall, therefore, look for possible alternative explanations for cited findings.

Without drawing too rigid a distinction, it may be useful to divide environmental factors in the elicitation of aggressive behaviors into permanent and temporary ones. The first are values that more or less consistently are transmitted by culture and that affect the normative manner in which members of the culture will learn to deal with various classes of situations. We have already said that some individuals become more or less chronically aggressive, others lead substantially nonaggressive lives, and still others seem to elicit aggression from other individuals. Keeping these differences in mind, it is nevertheless possible to compare cultures and subcultures with regard to the degree to which stress is laid upon aggressive behavior. This observation becomes particularly cogent when we consider obvious differences, such as those pertaining to sex, for instance. In our culture, boys are obviously taught and encouraged to use aggressive, "assertive," or "competitive" behavior to a far greater degree than are girls. A boy is encouraged to "stand up for himself," and not to let anyone "push him around"; in some instances, even to be a "scrapper," or a "fighter." For girls this is true to a far lesser degree. Looking across cultures, we also find some anthropological studies indicating that certain cultures discourage aggressive behavior to a remarkable degree, while others seem to place a great premium upon it (see, for instance, Benedict's [1946] comparison between the Pueblo and the Dobu cultures).

The history of our civilization, as it is taught in most elementary and intermediate schools, is often little more than a compendium of violence, warfare, and aggression, which is offered not in a spirit of disapproval, discouragement, or despair, but rather as a glorification of great military leaders and ruthless political figures. Men genuinely dedicated to nonviolence, if they are discussed at all, certainly fall into the classification of a minority group. Yet, while we teach our children the importance of man's military exploits, we attempt at the same time to imbue them with democratic values and respect for the self-determination of others. Our education of the child thus engenders an unavoidable conflict of values in him. When confronted by a decision, he may be totally perplexed as to whether his society, as well as his conscience, call for an aggressive or a conciliatory response.

An experiment by Berkowitz and LePage (1967) provides a striking example. They exposed people to insult while on a table before the subjects lay various neutral objects for one condition, and weapons, such as a pistol, for the other. The individuals who saw the aggressive instruments before them responded more violently than the others, even though their purely verbal aggression could not and did not utilize those weapons. In other words, the mere presence of aggressive instruments seems to enhance even those types of aggression which do not utilize those instruments at all. It is not easy to explain these findings either in terms of a purely situational theory, or in terms of personality, ignoring the situation. The most economical statement would have to assert that particular situational characteristics elicit and energize learned habits to a greater or lesser degree.

The immediate social environment in which a person finds himself at a moment of potential aggression may well influence his decision toward selecting the aggressive response. For instance, a group of which the person is a member, and which is involved in the situation together with the person, may convey to him very definite views as to how he should act. However, it could be wrong to assume that a group is effective in producing or enhancing aggression only by directly pressuring a person to commit aggression "against his will." Findings by Thibaut (1950) and by Pepitone and Reichling (1955) showed that highly cohesive or tightly knit groups aggressed more strongly against an insulting outsider than groups with a low degree of cohesiveness, that is, less tightly knit. Again real-life analogies readily come to mind: a high degree of solidarity in a platoon, in a club, or even in a juvenile gang produces a high degree of helping behavior for the members of the group, and hostility and aggression against threatening outsiders.

A famous series of studies by Lewin, Lippitt, and White (1939) shows that the political climate in which a group functions also affects the degree of resistance it opposes to an insulting outsider. Children showed greater spontaneous solidarity in resisting an adult who tried "to push them around" when they had previously experienced "democratic" leadership by an adult group leader than when that leadership had been autocratic or passive. Berkowitz (1964) perceptively categorized the types of social support of aggression into "emotional" and what might be called "cognitive" ones. An example of emotional support might be the group's cheering the aggressor on; cognitive support is exemplified by information or instructions conveyed by other group members, such as telling the attacker something that makes the victim more deserving of punishment.

The importance of the phenomenological effects of the total stimulus situation on the potential aggressor cannot be exaggerated. Perhaps it would not be amiss to emphasize promptly that the statement does not remove the study of individual acts from the realm of experimental psychology. It has long been realized that the purely physical correlates of a stimulus have little meaning, psychologically, except perhaps in the more basic reflex and operant processes. The letters S-T-O-P have a certain predictable meaning for the literate adult, which nevertheless is quite independent of the specific manner in which the letters have been executed. The insistence that a stimulus must be "evaluated" does not, then, mean that such evaluation is beyond rigorous inquiry. It only implies that we cannot rely upon a physical description of the stimulus to allow a total and error-free prediction of aggressive behavior Therefore, Pepitone's approach (1964) begins with a finer analysis of the "threat" stimulus, postulated by Maslow (1941) and Rosenzweig (1944). "Threat" may be classified into the thwarting of various needs, such as "status," or "affiliation," but it may also consist of a threatened loss of self-esteem, or it may be simply a strong external pressure toward acting as others do. It is not difficult to think of everyday parallels: the unintentional slight is resented less than the obviously intended insult. More specifically, Pepitone (1958) showed that an instigator's greater or lesser reponsibility for his act, the justifiability of it, and the intentionality with which it was committed affected the degree of resentment by the victim of the slight (see also Pastore, 1952). Magaziner (1961) found that hostility against an insulting person lessened after the insulted person's self-worth had been enhanced. An apology by the original instigator, but also praise or flattery by a third party, may readily decrease aggressive tendency.

SPECIAL EFFECTS IN THE PROPAGATION OF BEHAVIORS IN CROWDS OR GROUPS

Redl and Wineman (1962) speak of the "contagion" of behavior. This intriguing, but mysterious, notion has some appeal for the psychologist. Wheeler (1966) defines it as behavior in which the subject is normally motivated to engage, but against which there are barriers or inhibitions. Observation of others leads to "contagion," in that inhibitions or barriers are lessened. The concept is a different one from those which ascribe to the model the role of teaching new behaviors or inducing in the observer increased motivation to perform already learned behaviors. "Contagion" assumes that the motivation to execute this behavior is already high, but that the execution is inhibited by the expectation of punishment or censure.

The effects of the model here would be due not to an increase in motivation, but rather to a decrease of the restraining factors. In order for this effect to occur, the model need not be attractive, and need receive no reward for his behavior; although, of course, if the model is punished, it would be unlikely that inhibitions against the behavior would be removed in the observer.

Wheeler and Levine (1967) further showed that the characteristics of a model are of considerable importance, in a rather nonobvious fashion. Naively, for instance, one would predict that if the model is perceived by the observer as being highly similar to himself, imitation would be more likely than if the model is perceived as being dissimilar or remote, because such similarity should make it easier for the observer "to identify" with the model. The authors, however, found the very opposite: The dissimilar model was imitated more in terms of aggressive behavior than the similar model. The authors explain their findings by asserting that our society has strong restraints against aggressive behavior, and that where a dissimilar model was observed to break these restraints, transgression was perceived as more generally acceptable than when a similar model had transgressed.

The effects of groups may work also in the opposite direction. For instance, Kaufmann and Feshbach (1963a) found that fictitious group norms emphasizing nonaggressive responses to provocation led to less aggressive behavior after instigation than the absence of these norms. A subsequent study by the same authors (1963b) established that this decrease was not due to simple inhibition or fear. Two communications were devised: Although both deprecated aggressive behavior, the "inhibitory" communication stressed the sinfulness and moral unacceptability of aggressing and the retribution that would surely follow; the "rational" communication stressed a constructive, mature attitude as an alternative preferable to aggression, and mentioned no punishment. The inhibitory appeal produced displaced aggression in habitually hostile subjects; but the constructive, rational appeal, stressing nonaggressiveness, produced no such displacement. In addition, where these subjects had been instigated, they showed considerable task disruption on a perceptual skill task, unless, again, they had received a rational communication appealing, as it were, to their better nature rather than threatening guilt and stressing the unacceptability of aggression.

We have already seen that the presence of emotional arousal does not imply that aggression will occur. There is evidence, first of all, that "anger" does not appear to be a physiologically unique state, and that the name given to an arousal state may depend upon situational cues. But even when a person "feels angry," aggression does not necessarily follow. For instance, Hokanson and Shetler (1961) found that physiological arousal in human adults (the measure used was systolic blood pressure) produced by another person's insults (and, one would surmise, readily termed "anger" by the persons so instigated, as well as by a casual observer) could be reduced by aggression, as is hypothesized by the Frustration-Aggression hypothesis. However, withdrawal by the insulting person was equally effective, provided that retaliatory aggression was perceived as "inappropriate," that is, if the instigator was a person of allegedly high status. In other words, the subjects quickly "got over" insults by "important" people without having committed aggression, presumably because they had not learned in the past that in such a situation they had to redeem their honor by aggressing. These findings once more indicate that the meaning of "frustration" is inseparable from the cognitive evaluations that are so crucial in understanding interpersonal aggression.

The most startling series of findings relating to social influence and aggression (although the author prefers to call it "obedience") was obtained by Milgram (1963, 1964, 1965). His experiments are original enough to deserve a description in some detail:

A person comes to the laboratory and, under the pretext that he and another person are taking part in a learning experiment, he is told to give increasingly severe electric shocks to that other person. (The other person is a confederate who does not really receive any shocks, but convincingly, simulates distress.) The experimenter induces the subject to step up the shock intensity to a level marked "Danger: Severe Shock." The purpose of the experiment is to determine the point at which the subject refuses to comply with the experimenter's instructions.

The results of the first experiment (1963) showed that American adult males of average or higher intelligence were far less likely than had been expected to defy the experimenter's authority by refusing to commit what clearly appeared to be a reprehensible, possibly dangerous act. Although descriptions of the procedure given previously to the experimenter's colleagues and psychology majors had yielded the unanimous prediction that all but a negligible percentage of subjects would refuse to continue in the face of the "helpless" "learner's" protests, it was found that almost two thirds of the subjects eventually delivered a shock labeled "extremely painful and dangerous." Later studies demonstrated that group pressure can achieve the same obedience as an authoritarian source (Milgram, 1964), or facilitate disobedience to an authoritarian source (Milgram, 1965).

The uniqueness of these studies consists not in the processes themselves; conformity and obedience are phenomena well-known in the literature. However, even the most passionate believers in the effectiveness of interpersonal influence would not have predicted the high percentage of "conformers" in this ostensibly critical situation.

A subsequent series of studies by the author (Kaufmann, 1968) showed that the great majority of college students who are peripheral accessories ("bystanders") in a similar situation do not even attempt minimal steps to interrupt or terminate the proceedings. As in Milgram's case, these subjects also based their compliance upon the ostensible demand characteristics of the alleged "learning experiment."

These findings constitute powerful support for the thesis that aggressive acts often occur more as a function of situational demands than of intrapersonal traits. Arendt (1963), in a discussion of Nazi atrocities, suggests that Nazi sadism derived more from simple banality than from "inner states" such as aggressive drives, anti-Semitism, and so on.

To sum up, the processes whereby a child acquires aggressive tendencies have been studied both in a natural setting and in experimental situations. As in many other areas of the study of human behavior, both methods have obvious advantages and drawbacks. Naturalistic studies have had to rely almost exclusively upon parents' self-report about their own ways of raising children, although some inferences have been drawn from pervading norms of specific subcultures and socioeconomical strata. On the other hand, experimental studies, although affording opportunities for precisely controlled conditions, inevitably use models who are "artificial" in the sense that they are not the parents of the child. Also, experimental manipulations are of short duration, and little can be said about generalization with regard to the child's observed behavior. Quite similar reservations apply, of course, to the study of adult aggression.

The pervasiveness of aggression is readily explainable if we consider that almost everyone in our society has opportunities to learn how to engage in aggressive behaviors and is often rewarded for such behavior. Not only are weapons and fists discovered to have appropriate uses, but subtler skills of insult and derogation soon become familiar to the developing child. There is, thus, hardly anyone in our society of whom it can be said that he is unacquainted with aggression. The emission or performance of aggressive acts, however, is subject to social influences in innumerable ways.

THE MASS MEDIA AS TRANSMITTERS OF SOCIAL NORMS AND AS ELICITORS OF AGGRESSION

It should not come as a surprise that the effects of mass media, especially television, have elicited widespread concern regarding their effects upon children. The most telling attack against much of the violence that animates popular reading matter and, more recently, television viewing has come from Wertham (1954, 1966). Wertham has conducted a long, courageous, and brilliant fight against the philosophy of those who advocate violent and cruel entertainment for children, ostensibly because this allows children to vent or release their "aggressive drive" harmlessly. Needless to say, the purveyors of this philosophy are frequently those who produce comic books, television programs, or toys that base their appeal upon their violent, aggressive, or warlike nature. Wertham argues that to see cruel acts performed, not only by criminals, but even by individuals supposedly on the side of the law must lead to a coarsening of a child's sensibilities or, to use the psychologist's language, they provide models which convey the acceptability of aggression. In addition, being exposed to toys that are replicas of instruments of destruction, and even of torture, as well as to statements, philosophies, and instruments that in part advocate or condone such behaviors, or—and this is perhaps even more nefarious—being encouraged to view such behaviors with indiffer ence, as being "part of human nature," must in turn engender a greate readiness to accept such events, not only as an inevitable aspect of the human condition, but indeed, as a frequently desirable method of resolvin disputes. The child cannot help but learn from these powerful socializin agents that aggression, torture, and murder are acceptable aspects c human interaction. War, too, in this manner, becomes just a commonplace unavoidable, and perhaps even an adventuresome aspect of, human life.

This gratuitous and rationalized violence pervades many movies and TV programs of the "family" variety. Indeed, it could be argued (though Wertham does not so argue) that comic books animated with unusua cruelty, which existed in a largely clandestine fashion in the forties and fifties, have now become an accepted, integral part of family entertain ment. Now, it is true that Wertham does not adduce conclusive evidenc that such programs do indeed produce aggression, and perhaps delin quency, in growing people. But he does argue convincingly against thos who maintain that observing such aggression, or participating in aggres sive play, reduces or channels unavoidable aggressive drives. Why not then, Wertham asks, have programs and activities that allow a child t rechannel the (equally basic) sex drive through games that have rap or other forms of sexual activity for their topic?

We could go one step further and ask why most adults who ar concerned with the socialization of their children are so highly inconsisten in that they aprove of toy pistols, bombs, and flamethrowers and perm their children to watch programs in which people are habitually murdere or tortured, yet protest anxiously when these same children are expose to the relatively harmless picture of a nude woman. If we carry Wertham' argument to its logical conclusion, we should not only welcome hardcor pornography as desirable reading and television material; we should als advocate a burgeoning of sex and "rape" games, peddled insinuatingl by Captain Kangaroo and Romper Room. By thus "draining off" sexu drive, children and adolescents would not only refrain from criminal "se acts," but would be spared also much of the turbulence occurring durin puberty.

Another psychiatrist who has expressed intense concern about mod rn toys that imitate wholesale weapons of destruction is Dr. Carl Kline. n an issue of the *Progressive* (1966) he notes that such toys do not neet the basic requirements of a good toy: they are not creative, they each nothing constructive. Apparently Dr. Kline does subscribe to the otion that aggressive outlets are necessary for the emotional health of he child. But even so, he maintains that these toys do not represent useful outlet for aggression, because they do not permit the child to xpress his "real hostilities." Finally, Dr. Kline maintains that war toys o not introduce the child to a realistic view of adult life. For while ar is at present a fact of life, it is also an extremely unpleasant and regrettable one. It would follow, therefore, from Dr. Kline's argument, nat to make this dreadful and, it is to be hoped, remediable fact of fe appear pleasant and agreeable is highly unrealistic. He concludes is exhortation with a flat statement: "People who learn to play non-iolently as children, can learn to live non-violently as adults."

One is struck by the observation that no study has yet been attempted elating parents' overall aggressiveness and their attitudes toward war, oward the possession of war toys, toward horror comics, and toward ermissiveness in the television and movie-viewing habits of their children. s it conceivable that some children are exposed to these influences, not ecause they so demand, but because they are rewarded and encouraged y their parents who themselves enjoy such activities? There is a close nalogy between this possibility and the widely caricatured parent who uys his son a toy train and plays with it himself.

It might be useful at this point to differentiate much of this type f entertainment from older traditions of literature and play in which eath, disease, injury, and war are not unknown. Clearly, the *Iliad* affords rather frightening panorama of what man can do to his fellowman. here is, however, a basic difference between violence presented in that ontext and the mindless atrocities inflicted by a comic book hero or by a good guy" in a television serial. Hercules, Hector, and Manelaus were uperhuman hero figures. There was little danger of the average Greek, specially the Greek child, identifying himself with such a figure and eing himself as excuting similar deeds. Today, too, *King Lear, Hamlet,* r the *Odyssey* can be read and cherished as major works of art in which eath, violence, and even cruelty form an integral part of the drama. hese writings are, in a sense, morality literature, in that the characters mbolize and abstract the turbulence of human fate.

On the other hand, in a modern television program both outlaws nd those charged with enforcing the law indulge in habitual violence. he observer, especially when he is an impressionable child, may well iew the activities of the personages as commonplace and perhaps even raiseworthy. He may quite easily "identify" with the individuals, a process aat is unlikely to occur with the personages in *King Lear* or in the

Odyssey. He may do so for at least two reasons: (a) because the observer characters become for him models whose attainments and powers he ad mires, and (b) because even minimal attempts at copying some of their behaviors may indeed lead to unexpected reward. For instance, threatenin a playmate with a weapon or punching him in the stomach may ear him various rewards, such as the facile admiration of his playmates.

Even though the evidence is not conclusive at this point, it is cer tainly strong enough to warrant a second look at much of what passe for entertainment and games in our society. Also, there is ample evidenc that not only people, but also other organisms come to accept moderatel uncomfortable or painful stimuli when they are presented frequentl enough, and especially when they are accompanied by other, pleasar experiences. For instance, cats can learn to approach a painful shock giving every evidence of well-being, provided that the shock in the pas has been paired with food. People can come to accept as commonplacc situations that were previously regarded with horror. There is much anec dotal evidence in the literature of how readily a European living in Indi or China accepts everyday manifestations of previously inconceivable pov erty and the monstrous disfigurements deliberately inflicted upon childre destined for the occupation of begging. Also, few of us are unaware tha to German and Allied military personnel during World War II, event that were previously inconceivable soon became quite acceptable whe observed, and sometimes were readily perpetrated by the heretofor squeamish observer.

It is true that we cannot reject offhand the possibility that the fantas behavior evoked by watching certain fictitious "action" programs help at least some individuals to release some energy that might otherwis result in the type of hyperactivity that often results in aggression. Fc instance, Feshbach (1967) found that boys residing in an institution fc boys exhibited less interpersonal aggression when exposed to a customar fare of violent TV shows than did another group watching nonvioler programs. No such differences were found for noninstitutionalized boy. It could well be, of course, that the institutionalized boys no longer neede to *learn* aggression from TV shows, but reacted with annoyance to "boring" substitute for their usual programs. Nevertheless, the possibl need for drive-reducing fantasy behavior for some individuals require further investigation. Even if it were found to be the case, however, would constitute a weak argument against the findings and argumen presented above. Also, the admonition that all the data are not yet i is of little help. Perhaps, we cannot afford to wait for all the evidenc to be in. Our society is subject to ever-increasing stress; economic an racial unrest are rampant. It need not be argued that our troubles ste from a greater acceptance of casual violence in the environment of ou children. Perhaps such acceptance is the *result* of the turmoil existin n our society, engendered by very real crises and changes imposed upon us by many factors, such as technological advances, changes in religious outlook, population growth, changes in communication facilities, and so on. However, the growing child—and also the adult (because adults too are continuously socialized; that is, they too adopt norms and behavior patterns from their society, and especially from such authoritative sources as communications media)—*learn* their value system. Once we have discarded the alleged usefulness of violent entertainment and war games as a "lightning conductor" for otherwise dangerous aggression, there is really no very good reason left why the prospect of war, torture, and murder should be made an object of amusement and entertainment for the child.

Without making any grandiose generalization, the reader, having come thus far in our discussion, might share with the writer some uneasiness over the tendency of our society to build into its members two kinds of values: those that favor aggressive behavior in a relatively wide class of situations, and those that disapprove of and inhibit such behavior, except perhaps in a very narrow class of rather unequivocal situations. At worst, such a course might well lead to callousness and indifference in the face of human suffering; and a readiness to inflict it. The least that might be expected is a confusion of the values relating to man's behavior toward his fellowman.

VII

Prejudice and Discrimination

Early studies of prejudice are examined. What is the usefulness of
the Frustration-Aggression hypothesis toward an understanding of
prejudice? Prejudice is learned in several ways, such as learning
specific prejudices; learning the style or tendency toward prejudiced
thinking; going along with the prejudices of others. What are some
personality characteristics related to prejudiced thinking? It is
suggested that existing prejudice facilitates eventual aggression.
Victims of prejudice may develop special personality and behavioral
characteristics such as self-aggression. Antagonisms among groups
victimized by prejudice may mirror the prejudices of the dominant
majority. Interactions between prejudiced individuals and targets of
prejudice play an important part in determining what form the
expression of prejudice will take, and how the targets of prejudice
will respond.

T HE PRESENT CHAPTER bears a strong relationship to the preceding one
Here too we are concerned with situations in which attack or aggression
of various types evolves. However, the present topic is sufficiently impor
tant to warrant separate treatment. Also, it has perhaps enlisted more pas
sions, and therefore more misconceptions, than the more transitory, situa
tional aspect of aggression.

In 1950 a major work undertook to examine the personality charac
teristics of prejudiced individuals. *The Authoritarian Personality* (Adorno
Frenkel-Brunswik, Levinson, & Sanford, 1950) proceeded from the basi
hypothesis that various, not obviously germane aspects of personality func
tioning were related by virtue of their symbolic similarity. Thus a preju
diced person, inclined to view "outsiders" with suspicion or hate, woul
also show this suspicion of the new or unknown in his political, economic
and aesthetic views.

Although the work was widely criticized because of a number c methodological flaws (Christie & Jahoda, 1954), its major shortcoming lies in the almost nonexistent consideration of group norms, and, more generally, the enormous "pull" of specific situational determinants. After having discussed in considerable detail our grounds for favoring a social learning theory of aggression in general, there should be little need to emphasize that prejudice and its behavioral correlate, discrimination, are in the opinion of the writer, also viewed most economically as the results of experiences the individual undergoes in his lifetime. We still remember with embarrassment and shame how easily the stimulus qualities of an Oriental physiognomy elicited both a strongly aversive emotion and a readiness for unbridled aggression on the part of many of us some years ago. Within a society, too, more or less subtle processes may serve to brand members of a given ethnic or religious group as suitable targets for aggression by the majority. As distinct, then, from "undifferentiated" aggression, prejudice refers to habitual antagonism, frequently coupled with a readiness to aggress, against members of a certain national or ethnic group.

Studies have been undertaken of the personality dynamics of individuals obsessed with a high degree of group hatred, and the manner in which such attitudes might be prevented or cured. Put somewhat differently, questions are asked about the basic differences between people tending toward liberal, democratic attitudes and those favoring authoritarian, intolerant systems. It is relevant to point out that this difference is often viewed as a dichotomy, much on the lines of early western films, with liberal heroes on one side and antidemocratic villains on the other. Thus, over the last two decades a number of more or less inspired studies have appeared which attempted to find predictive and correlated variables identifying the personality structure of the fanatic hater (Hoffer, 1958; Sartre, 1948). Our purpose, however, lies not with extreme instances of pathology. Rather than view the world as populated by two kinds of people, authoritarians and liberals, it might be more appropriate to consider a society as being composed of individuals whose behaviors and attitudes can assume, under properly conducive conditions, widely different forms of mutual respect or intolerance.

THE FRUSTRATION-AGGRESSION HYPOTHESIS AND THE "SCAPEGOAT"

The issue of prejudice has also been examined in the context of the Frustration-Aggression hypothesis, discussed in Chapter III. For instance, the original proponents (Dollard et al., 1939) viewed persecution against Jews in Germany and Negroes in the United States as engendered by economic frustrations and displaced from the true sources of frustration upon more accessible and weaker targets such as are presented by Negroes and Jews. In Germany the post-World War I inflation and unemployment were seen as the primary cause; here in the United States, Hovland and Sears (1940) found an interesting inverse relationship between the size of the yearly cotton crop and the number of lynchings in the South, where these crops were until recently the principal source of wealth.

This notion of the "scapegoat" asserts that a prejudiced individual selects certain groups as objects of contempt and hate because he sees them as being responsible for his misfortunes. The ancient notion of the scapegoat forms part of the lore of a number of religions: The human sacrifice in some instances, the expiatory fowl of the Jews, and, finally, the Redeemer in Christianity are seen as taking on the sins of others, thereby liberating them from punishment.

From this line of reasoning, it is only a simple step to ensure expiation by not waiting for supernatural vengeance but by perpetrating it directly. Thus, we have come full circle—from early, "barbarous" human sacrifices, through the expiatory fowl of the Jews, and through the divinely appointed, but conscious, assenting Redeemer—to the scapegoat who is punished so that we may go free.

However appealing this poetic exercise, its explanatory and predictive usefulness is quite limited. As was the case with the Frustration-Aggression hypothesis examined earlier, the antecedent-consequent relationship, whose discovery must be the serious investigator's ultimate aim, is once again quite nebulous; and the temptation to engage in circular reasoning is considerable: he that holds prejudices must be hounded by frustrations, and the unfortunate who is subjected to frustrations must develop prejudices, no matter how recondite. Also, as Klineberg (1950) points out, acts of violence against other groups do not necessarily occur in societies in which the likelihood of individual frustration is greater. More important, Sherif and Sherif (1965) argue cogently that it makes no sense to extrapolate from the motivational urges and frustrations of an individual to behaviors in a group or society because in a group or society interaction processes and reciprocal influences play a powerful part. On the basis of this and earlier arguments, the notion of a one-to-one relationship between frustration and aggression is dismissed also in the context of prejudice and intergroup conflict, not because it has been conclusively disproved, but because it has been found inaccurate, inadequate, or unparsimonious in the explanation and prediction of behavior.

Once again we are forced to look for a theory that goes beyond invariant processes based upon alleged drives and physical stimulus similarities. It might be reasonable to hypothesize, for instance, that a substitute target is frequently chosen because attack upon it might serve to restore the aggressor's self-esteem (White & Lippitt, 1960).

Thus, in this brief examination we shall neglect the search for likely origins of that most pervasive of myths—the myth of "race"; it has been dealt with, and disposed of as a meaningful determinant of behavioral differences, by a number of scholars (Benedict, 1943; Montagu, 1963; Pettigrew, 1964; Barzun, 1965). Instead, we shall focus upon prejudice in the following contexts:

- Learning specific prejudices
- Learning the "style" of prejudiced thinking
- Going along with the prejudices of others
- Some personality characteristics related to prejudiced thinking
  Prejudice as a facilitator of aggression
- The effects of being the objects of prejudice upon aggressive and aggression-eliciting behavior

In sum, our study of prejudice limits itself to the development of prejudice and the relationship between prejudice and aggression. In considering this relationship we shall, once again, focus on the holder of prejudiced views, the target of these views, and situational variables affecting the interaction between the two participants. Needless to say, such an approach is in no way meant to assign the respective roles permanently; the target of one prejudice may in turn hold prejudices of his own, either against members of the groups who hold him in contempt or against third parties.

LEARNING SPECIFIC PREJUDICES

It is, first of all, necessary to establish the distinction between acquiring the emotional and cognitive habits favoring prejudiced functioning, and learning to view a particular group with disfavor.

As Horowitz (1936) noted a number of years ago, anti-Negro prejudice tends to be unrelated to personal experiences, and to depend instead upon social influences. Although some cases of an aversive emotional response that is truly classically conditioned could probably be cited, it is quite safe to consider these instances as rare. The emotional aversion experienced by some individuals upon contact with members of certain groups is probably mediated symbolically, in the sense that the stimulus person is, in the beholder's imagination, endowed with noxious qualities.

Williams (1964) maintains that a certain amount of intergroup prejudice does not express a specific ethnic dislike so much as a kind of generalized timidity and feeling of awkwardness in coping with unfamiliar situations and unknown people. Thus, a person might say "I feel a bit uneasy in the company of Negroes." It could be maintained, though, that this argument begs the question. Unless these feelings have been previously learned, why should a white accountant, who let us say, has brown eyes, black hair, and a straight nose, feel such uneasiness in the presence

of an accountant of minimal African ancestry, who may, moreover, resem
ble him in many ways—as people with similar occupations are wont to
do—and yet experience no discomfort with a "white" pharmacist with
blue eyes, brown hair, a turned-up nose, and no interests in common
Indisputably, some people more than others prefer the company of other
individuals with whom they have a common interest, but a relatively un
prejudiced person will make such a selection on the basis of relevant
rather than irrelevant, characteristics. If he wishes to discuss deep-sea
fishing, he will do so comfortably with a person of similar interests, rather
than with a confirmed oceanophobe. But another conversation partner
may be preferred if the conversation topic shifts to, say, Beethoven's
piano sonatas.

Another mechanism may also be operative: an individual is rein
forced for exhibiting behaviors *indicating* aversion, such as shuddering
grimacing, and so on, and these behaviors may gain in strength because
they are now part of an operant conditioning process. Furthermore, the
acquisition of overt, voluntary behaviors indicating prejudice, such as mak
ing derogatory statements, is readily derivable from the higher learning
processes discussed in Chapters V and VI. Specifically, the processes of
imitation or an identification with a model are clearly applicable, respec
tively, to expressions of prejudice against a particular group, and to adopt
ing the peculiar cognitive style of the highly prejudiced person. Presumably
specific instances of imitation would precede the more abstract process
of "prejudiced thinking." Children are often heard to derogate specific
groups, but rarely give expression to a general philosophy of intergroup
antagonism or xenophobia. Stereotypes, which Klineberg (1965) call
"pictures in our heads," furthermore assume a considerable degree of
consistency within a given culture and about specific groups. For instance
Katz and Braly (1933) found remarkable consistency across various
American college populations in the characteristics of certain ethnic group
and in the "desirability" ranking given them. Sometimes the tendenc
to indulge in faulty stereotyping or stimulus generalization leads to com
pletely nonsensical results. For instance, in an experiment by Razran
(1950), the subjects evaluated girls' pictures without names in terms of
beauty, likability, character, and so forth. Two months later, the same
individuals evaluated the same pictures again. But this time some of the
pictures bore Jewish or Italian names; others had Irish or Anglo-Saxon
names. Jewish and Italian names resulted in a substantial drop of liking
and some decrease in ratings of beauty and character. On the other hand
especially for "Jewish" girls, an increase in attributed ambition occurred
In a study by Schoenfeld (1942), students were asked to attribute person
ality characteristics to unknown persons, purely on the basis of their given
names. For instance, "Richard," it was widely agreed, must be handsome
"Herman" must be stupid, and so forth.

The notion of the "kernel of truth," or "where there is smoke there is fire," often adduced by prejudiced persons to account for their feelings, is equally irrational. It is surely meaningless to discover a miserly Jew, or an unwashed Negro, and use them as evidence of "racial" characteristics. Before it would make sense to explore the grounds of such characteristics, one would have to ask whether the "representative" individuals are indeed representative; that is, how great a percentage they represent, and whether the rate of incidence is actually greater than that for otherwise comparable members of the allegedly "superior" group.

Williams (1947) has suggested that "visibility" is a determinant factor in a minority group's becoming a target of prejudice. In some respects, this is surely accurate. An obscure category, being known to few and relevant to none, can hardly become a satisfactory object of blame and contempt; its members are simply "not there" often enough to remind the prejudiced persons of their "noxious" existence. In a way, however, the stipulation of "visibility" can easily become tautological, since the very descriptions of the "visible" group may imply a subtle, perhaps socially sanctioned, negative attitude. Thus, the Jews are "visible" in New York, where they constitute a relatively large proportion, and they are "visible" in a rural setting because they are a small minority. In sum, they are "visible" wherever someone makes a point of singling them out for observation.

The particular brand of pseudo-logic or psycho-logic involved in prejudice is by no means limited to attitudes toward members of another group. Prejudiced, superficial, or irrational behavior can be observed in many contexts; but usually its consequences are slight, and in most instances limited to the person holding such beliefs. Take an example of a person who once ate a lobster and subsequently became ill. Usually he does not ask himself whether the particular lobster was of a bad quality or poorly prepared, whether he perhaps became ill as a consequence of having eaten something else, whether he might have contracted a virus infection which had nothing to do with anything he had eaten, or even whether an expectation of the lobster making him ill engendered enough autosuggestive symptoms to produce such illness. He might even go so far as to say, "Perhaps I should not become ill if I ate lobster again, but why take chances? I am better off not exposing myself to this risk again" (Kaufmann, 1966).

All of these attitudes are to a greater or lesser degree irrational, and for every one of them a parallel could be found accounting for a person's prejudiced behavior toward members of another group. Notice, however, that in both instances we assume some at least *latent* misgivings (or prejudices) toward lobsters (or members of the particular group). It might not even occur to our hypothetical gourmet to question the quality of, say, a salad, an apple, or a potato he had eaten at the same time, simply because, for no very good reason, he did not entertain similar misgivings about those rather commonplace foods as he did about the exotic and unusual lobster. He was what we might call playing it safe with regard to foods because in some way or other he had learned that the unaccustomed is likely to lead to trouble.

Correspondingly, we will find many individuals practicing discrimination who upon interrogation would show no powerful prejudices, but will simply cite, in a seemingly reasonable fashion, the respective subjective probabilities they hold with regard to anticipated unpleasant experiences with "individuals like themselves" as opposed to members of the minority group against which they practice discrimination. They may say: "I quite agree that not all Negroes (Jews) are objectionable. Indeed, some of my best friends are Negroes (Jews)." "But," they will continue, "it is much more likely that among the Negroes or Jews I meet there will be somebody objectionable than there would be likely among people like myself" (Kaufmann, 1966). They may also go on to cite the likelihood of causing embarrassment to their friends or "other customers" by bringing them in contact with a member of the minority group. They may even assert that they themselves hold no prejudices at all, but that their friends unfortunately, do not happen to see things in the same way.

The individual, in other words, grows up in a social world with norms; one class of these norms concerns attitudes and behaviors toward members of specific other groups and, to some degree, toward all individuals who do not belong to the in-group. In Sherif and Sherif's (1964) term, the individual adopts these values, as well as others, from his "reference group," that is, from those groups (or individuals) upon whom he patterns himself in a positive (i.e., matching) or negative (i.e., contrasting) way. These reference groups are able to exert pressure in varying degrees depending both upon the susceptibility of the individual and the power the group has over him in terms of its ability to administer or withhold rewards and punishments of various kinds. The more a person is attracted to a group, the more influential its mores will be upon him. This was found by Festinger, Schachter, and Back (1950) in a communal housing development, and by Kelley and Volkart (1952) for boys belonging to the Boy Scouts.

Similarly, the status of the communicator enhances his persuasive power (Strodtbeck, James, & Hawkins, 1958; Kelman & Hovland, 1953). Pettigrew's (1959) work also corroborates this surmise: southern women who more strongly conformed to the social norms of church-going also had more intense anti-Negro attitudes.

Sometimes, when the individual does become exposed to a totally different set of norms, he will acquire these new norms with relative rapidity. Thus, Stouffer and his colleagues (1949) produced ample evidence to the effect that American soldiers from the South in World War II exhibited accepting attitudes toward Negro soldiers. These attitudes became more favorable as a direct function of contact with Negro soldiers. However, when these southern soldiers returned to their own environment at home, attitudes learned early in life regained the upper hand very quickly, and soon the soldiers became indistinguishable from their neighbors and friends, displaying customary prejudice against Negroes.

LEARNING THE "STYLE" OF PREJUDICED THINKING

As we have indicated above, the prejudiced individual may have learned not only to dislike certain groups in particular but also to favor the perceptual and reasoning processes that lead to stereotyping and prejudice in general. Therefore, it is hypothesized that the greater the person's previous tendency to engage in prejudiced thinking, the more sweeping will be his unwarranted inferences about a newly encountered group, or about one which, although it has been present all along, has only just become salient.

Suppose a person has formed certain stereotypes about Jews, among which we might expect such characteristics as "crafty businessmen," "unwilling to engage in manual labor," and "physical cowards." A story is told of an American who visited Israel, was most favorably impressed, but, at the same time, was quite puzzled. "Great," he said, "but where are all the Jews?" In all likelihood this individual (we would hope that he is a fictitious character) will not suddenly turn into a person who no longer thinks in stereotypes and clichés. More probably, he may have become a passionate pro-Semite who now attributes near-legendary qualities to the Jews, and perhaps compares that stereotype with an unfavorable one held with regard to another group. Similarly, an environmental situation, such as encountering a previously unknown group, is not seen as a *determinant* of prejudice—however unfortunate and recurring the relevant experience may be—but as a stimulus for eliciting established habits of stereotyping. It has been suggested (Bettelheim & Janowitz, 1950) that prejudice derives from threats to the self-esteem, as might occur when a person loses social status and income. But since we conceptualize tendencies toward holding prejudices as largely learned, we deem it fruitless to look for other personality characteristics as *causes* of prejudice. Instead, personality characteristics related to the tendency of making the kind of rash and unfavorable judgment, which we call prejudice, are seen as being learned as a result of those same experiences that produce the tendency itself.

It should be superfluous to point out the enormous difference between a realistic and reasoned use of data, and the entire fanciful inferences and generalizations that characterize prejudiced thinking. The argument that many stereotypes are false does not, of course, imply that all of them are false. Presumably, the stereotype that Watusis are darker skinned than Danes is almost universally applicable. Stereotyping is an indispensable form of generalizing from immensely varied perceptions and cognitions. The crucial distinction is not between the holding and not holding of stereotypes, but between flexibility and rigidity in the process of forming the categories indispensable for cognitive functioning. For instance, incontrovertible evidence can be cited to support the contention that the average Negro child scores lower on ability and achievement tests than his white counterpart. To deny this state of affairs out of fear that accepting it would be tantamount to joining ranks with racists or bigots is clearly absurd. To do so would negate all the efforts at correcting the wrongs that have been allowed to develop in our society.[1]

But a highly prejudiced person may use this same datum with a different understanding. Thus he might be readily inclined to ascribe these differences to innate racial deficiencies, partly, perhaps, because he would use the findings to make totally unwarranted inferences about other characteristics, and employ them in a manner deeply harmful to the Negro and (since injury to any part of our society surely impairs at least the moral well-being of all of us) to the entire society. The glaringly obvious caution that even the findings which show the greatest disparity still show a large overlap for the two populations would cut little ice. Nor would the validity of the instruments as predictors of specific outcomes be questioned. Pleading a concern for education, he would take these findings as grounds for segregation in the schools, without considering that to the extent that the effectiveness of the educational process is positively related to homogeneity in the classroom (and we are by no means sure to what extent this is the case), children should be grouped by ability rather than race. Controversies involving whites and blacks, however unrelated to the issue of interracial conflict, might tend to be perceived in terms of black-white confrontation, in which interests are irremediably polarized. A brilliant Negro would not be viewed as disconfirming the hypothesis of "innate" inferiority, but as "the exception which confirms the rule."

Such a person might also claim a great interest in eugenics, and use the argument of "racial inferiority" to inveigh against miscegenation. Of course, it is clear that to the degree that ability is genetically transmitted, the most intelligent offspring should result from unions between the brightest parents, regardless of their skin coloration.

To sum up, no one who has had occasion to observe prejudice

---

[1] There have been encouraging changes, especially where Negro children obtain greater exposure to varied environmental stimuli at an early age.

hinking would believe for a moment that if Negroes were to score significantly higher on all intelligence tests than any other group, prejudice
against them would disappear.

GOING ALONG WITH THE PREJUDICE OF OTHERS

But there is another process whereby a group can come to display
strong prejudice against a target group—a process that is simple, intuitively
obvious, and still has not entered into most of the experts' dealings with
prejudice. Suppose a small number of individuals who occupy an influential
or policy-making position in some group (political, ethnic, or whatever)
systematically direct derogation and threats toward members of another
group. It may well be that these few persons are passionately convinced
that the target group is a major threat to others. But even that assumption
is unnecessary; the hatemongers may simply find it expedient to unify
their followers by diverting their fears and hates for each other to a convenient outside target.

Now, we need only one further, quite minimal assumption—namely
that most or all of these followers, without accepting the propaganda
of the opinion leaders, simply do not *care* enough about the welfare of
the target group, or the abstract principle of the brotherhood of man,
to take a position contrary to that advocated. Then, if the advocates
of prejudice have a "program" that is appealing to their followers in
other ways, it may well be that their group, as a whole, may adopt an
intensely prejudiced policy, even though most group members are only
minimally prejudiced.

We can see, therefore, that the various ways in which a few opinion
makers can influence the attitudes and behaviors of a large number of
others make them potentially very dangerous. And it should at least give
pause to those who unthinkingly advocate "total and unrestricted freedom
of speech," even though all societies, no matter how honorably motivated,
have had to impose *some* type of limit. The exclusion of the right to
free speech when there is a "clear and present danger" of riot, or of
restraints against uttering threats, or of inflicting obscenities upon unwilling
others are instances in point. As I have argued elsewhere (Kaufmann,
1966), the determination of whether the self-serving or misguided utter-
ances of a few threaten a society (or a part of it) enough to warrant
its protection by depriving the inciters of their means of communication
must therefore be carefully determined by a judicial body in each case.
If existing laws are found powerless to extend suitable protection to the
members of its society, some legislative changes may result. It should
not surprise us, however, that automatic mouthings of a rule alleged to
be universal will not contribute much to the welfare of a complex society
riddled by problems and often subject to threats of internal strife.

SOME PERSONALITY CHARACTERISTICS RELATED TO PREJUDICED THINKING

Another consequence of a style of prejudiced thinking, as opposed to holding specific, unrelated prejudices, appears to be a general gratification of holding other people in contempt, merely by virtue of their belonging to the human species. The frequently found relationship between sweeping derogations of ethnic or national groups and lack of faith in human nature (Adorno et al., 1950) indicates that at least some form of prejudice is merely a type of concretization of a general dislike for one's fellowman. By ostensibly (but not totally) restricting disdain to a group from which one is different in at least one obvious respect, one reduces the implication of one's harsh judgment of others for oneself. Ascribing inferiority to others is rewarded by enhancing one's own worth without the trouble of having to show some worthwhile attainment. One might expect, therefore, that a general tendency to disparage other people or "human nature" (from which the critical person may consider himself, at least for present purposes, miraculously exempt) would be related to a tendency toward prejudice, although it is not necessary to assume the relationship to be a causal one. Such a relationship has been found directly to be the case in a study by Sullivan and Adelson (1954). Also, several studies have shown that the individual who is hostile, extrapunitive, or aggressive in his attitudes and everyday interactions also tends to hold negative attitudes about Jews (Lesser, 1958), expresses hostility toward a perceived out-group (Stagner, 1944), and perceives others to be hostile toward him (Murstein, 1961).

The degree of a person's overall "influenceability" (regardless of the origins of this characteristic) is likely to be of some importance. When we speak of a "prejudiced" individual, we surmise that he not only subscribes to certain derogatory simplifications about some other groups, but he will also be ready to accept new beliefs about groups previously unknown to him. There is evidence that persuasibility exists as a "content free" factor; that is, it exists independently of the subject matter of the type of appeal presented in any particular persuasive communication. Janis and Field (1959) demonstrated that an individual's susceptibility to persuasive communications dealing with one issue (e.g., "public participation in civil defense") is highly correlated with his susceptibility to persuasive communications about other issues (e.g., "the merits of a new television comedian").

It also appears that low self-esteem or a feeling of social inadequacy is a consistent characteristic of the individual showing high persuasibility. Janis (1954), Linton and Graham (1959), and Cohen (1959) have reported studies based upon both experiments and clinical histories which document this relationship, although investigators seem more successful in demonstrating the relationship with male than with female subjects. Festinger (1964) reports that the individual low in self-esteem is also less likely to investigate information that may be unfavorable to his existing attitudes or beliefs than an individual high in self-esteem.

The self-esteem variable, then, is one of particular significance, since low self-esteem is related to both persuasibility *and* insulation against contradictory views once an opinion has been found. This combination of factors is especially dangerous because it may decrease the effectiveness of counterpropaganda or attempts at education, once the persuasive communication has been received and assimilated.

The implications of these studies seem to be that overtly more hostile individuals are more difficult to influence, but typically hold attitudes particularly amenable to the formation of derogatory stereotypes. Contrary to what might intuitively be expected, education seems to be only minimally relevant. Thus Stember (1961) has quoted convincing evidence that more education does not imply less prejudice, even though the form and expression of prejudice vary across educational strata.

PREJUDICE AS A FACILITATOR OF AGGRESSION

Berkowitz and Holmes present ample evidence that previously existing dislike enhances the likelihood and intensity of displacing aggression upon the disliked individual (Berkowitz & Holmes, 1959, 1960). A subsequent study (Berkowitz & Green, 1962) showed that such displacement was selective: a previously disliked person was attacked more than a neutral one.

All this is not surprising, and is compatible with a social learning model. After all, "disliking" a person is at least in part comparable to "aggressing" against him. It would then readily follow that a target that has already elicited some type and degree of aggression will be more likely to elicit other forms of aggression, or simply more intense aggression of the original type, than a previously neutral stimulus.

The propaganda against another nation which often precedes war is an example of the systematic induction of those negative, generalized attitudes that constitute prejudice in order to facilitate or favor subsequent aggression. The long campaign of derogation, hate, and contempt against the Jews directed by a specifically appointed branch of the Nazi government to the German people certainly made it relatively easy to countenance the subsequently attempted genocide against them.

THE EFFECTS OF BEING THE OBJECTS OF PREJUDICE UPON AGGRESSIVE AND AGGRESSION-ELICITING BEHAVIOR

In the wake of the Brown Decision by the Supreme Court (1954), it is now common knowledge that prejudice and discrimination have severely deleterious effects upon the targets of such attitudes by a powerful majority. As Mead (1934) has emphasized, the child comes to know himself by "taking the role of the other," by seeing himself as he imagines others to see him. We know enough about the influence that can be exerted, particularly by "reference groups" (Sherif & Sherif, 1964; Newcomb, 1958), to expect that the attitudes and beliefs of a powerful and enviable majority group are likely to serve as models for groups having a lower status. Unfortunately, but not surprisingly, such attitudes and beliefs often have those same lower-status or minority groups for their objects.

In this manner, members of such minority groups, faced with what Festinger (1954) calls "social reality" institutionalized by the dominant majority, and frequently persuaded also by more or less subtle messages in the mass media, may develop a self-image that corresponds to a considerable degree with the views of the majority group. This self-picture tends to include a certain devaluation of self; that is, an acceptance of the majority group's judgment of inferiority.

For instance, Adelson (1953) found that some middle-class Jews look upon their lower-class coreligionists with no more favor than do many gentiles who could readily be classed as anti-Semites. These violators of middle-class standards are seen as brash, "pushy," and offensive. This is not to say that the gentiles fare any better; they are dichotomized into lower-class "anti-Semites" and middle-class "non-anti-Semites." Negro students have been found to give much the same description of "typical" Negroes as did white students, though with the addition of several more favorable traits to the list. Thus, the tendency for personality traits to fit the stereotype is an expression of acculturation to the beliefs and expectations of the majority (Bayton, 1941; Gilbert, 1951).

The derogatory stereotyping of their own and other minority groups can easily induce the types of self-aggression and antagonisms between minority groups which, at first sight, seem so unreasonable because they are so clearly maladaptive. In Lewin's (1948) chapter "Self-hatred Among Jews," he speaks of conflicts between the German or Austrian Jew and the East European Jews, and between the French Jew and the German Jew. This antagonism resulted from the conflictful situation of the semi-assimilated German and Austrian Jews, who saw their status threatened by the influx of other Jews, alien in culture and speech. This hatred may also be directed against Jewish institutions, Jewish mannerisms, or Jewish ideals. In one of the studies crucial in the Supreme Court decision (Clark & Clark, 1947) of Negro boys and girls between 3 and 7 years of age, the majority of the medium and dark children chose a Negro doll when asked an identification question ("Show me the doll that looks like you"). But, when asked a preference question ("Show me the doll that you like to play with"), 67 percent of the children chose the white doll.

These feelings of inferiority and of self-hatred, however, are seldom expressed in an unambiguous way. In what seems at first glance to be a contradiction, these attitudes may take the form both of in-group hatred and out-group identification, or of in-group solidarity and out-group hatred; even a general misanthropy and distrust toward other people might result. For instance, Johnson (1941) reported that in a study of over two thousand rural Negro boys and girls, there was a decided tendency for the same subjects to rate both black and white persons negatively. Lewin (1948) speaks of both the cohesive and disruptive forces in under-privileged groups. The members of such groups are hampered by their group affiliations; there are a number of reluctant members for whom the forces urging them away from the group are greater than the forces pulling them toward the group. On the other hand, because the minority group member's safety and security lie in his membership group, there is also a tendency to become uncritically favorable toward it (Allport, 1954). As Simpson and Yinger (1958) put it, "A feeling of common fate and shared problems exists alongside intragroup conflict and jealousy." A specific example illustrating some of these features is that of Negro anti-Semitism. Here we have in-group solidarity and out-group hatred in the banding together of Negroes against whites, and identification with the dominant out-group and its attitude by acceptance of anti-Semitism.

Another effect of living in a persistent state of social rejection may be that members of a minority group, in order to avoid even the shadow of suspicion that they suffer from certain character defect, assert that their behavior in that respect must be absolutely beyond reproach and far superior to that of the majority group. Thus a Jew may argue that Jews must be more ethical than gentiles in their business dealings, not because of a stricter code of ethics, but simply to forestall any possibility of an accusing finger being pointed against them. However, there is also considerable evidence that the opposite effect may obtain; that is, that the knowledge that one is perceived as a stereotype often results in one's living up to that stereotype. Merton (1949) calls this the self-fulfilling prophecy. A knows that B expects him to be, say, miserly, grasp-ing, and assertive, or if A is, say, an adolescent, rowdy and ill-mannered. Whenever A produces behaviors corresponding to B's expectations, B, though professing annoyance and dismay, in a subtle fashion also rewards A for having confirmed his, B's, beliefs, and thereby reinforces that be-havior pattern. The point is, of course, that both types of reactions repre-sent a "spurious" behavior syndrome in that the victim of prejudice cannot experience the more normal, less psychologically painful, processes of socialization.

The vicious cycle generated by such attitudes and behaviors was indicated by Myrdal (1944). His statement, revolutionary then, is almost self-evident in the light of today's greater psychological knowledge: Prejudice and discrimination must of necessity produce inferiority. Even though there are of course instances in which a few rare individuals are spurred on to exceptional effort and accomplishment, the disastrous effect upon the great majority, and not necessarily the less gifted persons, can no longer be denied. Stereotypes result in selective and distorted perception and, on the part of the stereotyped individual, may result in his living up to the stereotype, or reacting to it by behaving in an opposite extreme. These findings become even more critical if we consider that, as Allport (1954) has stated, stereotypes and subtle rejection have always preceded more overt acts of discrimination (and, frequently, direct aggression).

It is also not difficult to see that the antagonism displayed so readily by members of both groups is quite likely to reinforce already existing antagonisms. This, in effect, is another type of vicious cycle. Antagonism and expectation of the other person's objectionable qualities will most likely produce disagreeable or aggressive behavior; and since a disagreeable person is rarely liked, it will then be not at all difficult to rationalize and strengthen prejudices, which initially may have been merely abstract, as well as to justify eventual attack.

VIII

Aggression in International Relations

This chapter examines the applicability of our conceptualization of aggression to conflicts between nations. War has been viewed as being caused by the personal motives of national leaders, or by different national characters or interests. More recently, the psychoanalytic view is also a "personal" one; it considers not only the motives of leaders, but also of their followers. Although we no longer view war in such simplistic terms, psychology may be able to play a major role in controlling conflicts of interests among nations, and thereby eliminate wars. Perceptual distortions and breakdowns in communication intensify mutual distrust. And the personality of national leaders, though probably not the sole cause of a war, may certainly be a contributing factor. Thus, correcting misperceptions, encouraging communication, and a study of the personal ties of political figures should bring us closer to our goal.

In addition, we must learn more about the psychology of extreme stress, and the mechanisms whereby people readily learn to hate members of national groups whom only recently they had highly regarded. Finally, we know all too little about the cognitive processes whereby serious conflicts can be resolved by methods other than mindless violence.

*T*HE PRESENT BOOK is not a treatise in political science. Also, we shall not attempt here to present, or even discuss, detailed plans for a reduction of tension among nations in order that the likelihood of armed conflict may decrease. Remaining once more within the deliberately restricted framework of this study, we shall be concerned solely with the question whether psychology has something useful to say on the issue of conflict between nations.

Arguments against the barbarousness and futility of war are not new, though only in the past two decades or so have these become almost self-evident in that, in a total war, there could be no victory for the victor by any standards other than those of desperate or glorious self-immolation. Conceivably, this realization has produced a measure of restraint between the superpowers, which could destroy each other, rapidly and totally if armed conflict between them were to break out. Unfortunately, "lesser" wars are still very much of the present, and because actions among men are not governed solely by reason uncontaminated by hate, fear, or greed, the prospect of the ultimate absurdity, that of mutual annihilation, has not been banished.

PERSONAL AND IMPERSONAL CONCEPTUALIZATIONS OF WAR

Through history there can be observed a curious bipolar interpretation of the phenomenon of war. Thucydides and Plutarch are prime instances of psychological interpretations of warfare: they viewed the conflicts between nations as arising primarily from the motives of their leaders. Tacitus, though concerned with individual attributes, placed greater emphasis upon national character and conflict. Machiavelli was probably the first to attempt a synthesis between national interests and mass movements on the one hand and individual ambition on the other. But during the last century these two viewpoints diverged radically. Marxism emphasized economic interests to the total exclusion of individual motivation, whereas the psychoanalytic approach, though not necessarily excluding nonpsychological causes, stresses principally the individual motives of frustration, anxiety, and aggression. It is a "personal" or psychological interpretation which takes into account the motives not only of leaders but also of their followers. Even though Bernard (1957) may have restated the obvious when she pointed to incompatible goals and values as sources of conflict, many psychologists still view interpersonal and international strife as chiefly the product of frustration, and, from this premise, arrive at the unrealistic prediction that an elimination of "frustration" would bring universal harmony and peace.

The nationalistic or folkloric view has had its more recent adherents, too. Fascism and, to a greater degree, Nazism, drew heavily upon ethnic myths in order to claim for their "nation" (which was by no means always rigorously defined) such collective personal attributes as valor, anger, and vindictiveness. The putative attributes of a member of a nation so endowed corresponded to the avowed stereotype. In crass instances of noncorrespondence between an individual's behavior and what was expected of him, the national image was not broadened or rendered more flexible. Instead, he was accused of shameful deviancy, and, in many instances, publicly castigated.

A reexamination of the cogency of these diametrically opposed approaches has been undertaken by Klineberg (1965), Lasswell (1948), and Andreski (1964). They, and most other recent thinkers, reject a polarized interpretation, and prefer to allow for the contribution of individual as well as group variables in the initiation and maintenance of intergroup attitudes and behaviors, of which the psychological preparation for war, and the conduct of warfare, are a part.

We must recognize, first of all, that war is not an act arising from motives of interpersonal antagonism, even though interpersonal aggression is, of course, the inevitable result. The distinction becomes obvious when we consider that the military person who does most of the actual aggressing is not ordinarily motivated to protect himself or his family, or to gain spoils, to a greater degree than military personnel on a home base, or even civilians at home. Although by the definition given in Chapter I the combatant's behavior is classified as "aggressive," we shall expect little relationship between such personal antecedents as "frequency of reward for previous aggression" or "identification with an aggressive model" in childhood and subsequent valor or ferocity in battle.

Yet even if we guard against the simplistic fallacy of equating nations with men and attributing to the former emotions such as "anger" or "fear," it does not logically follow that international relations should remain the exclusive domain of political science and economics, and that psychology has nothing useful to contribute. After all, it is not nations who conduct war and mutilate and kill each other; it is people who assume the alleged identity of the nation (usually with little warrant) and project their own attitudes and emotions upon the passive and inarticulate nation. It is also people (though usually not the same who are mouthpieces for the nation's state of mind) who inflict injury and death upon each other for the purpose of preserving and furthering their country's "vital interest." At the very least, they "follow orders," even though without passionate convictions, and even though their effectiveness may be inferior to that of what Hoffer (1951) calls "the True Believer," such acquiescence is quite sufficient to destroy numerous lives.

Little further argument should therefore be required to support the contention that psychology cannot remain uninvolved in issues of international affairs. If it is assumed that the psychologist has any expertise at all (an assertion which we shall not argue here), then surely he cannot remove himself from that most crucial arena of interpersonal events.

What, then, are some useful contributions of psychology?

First of all, there exists a basic factor in the assessment of each government's motives and intentions by the other. Tuchman's brilliant book *The Guns of August* (1962) presents a horrifying picture of how self-deception and miscalculation pushed the world into World War I.

It is probably safe to surmise that the majority of wars originated not so much from a rational assessment of irreconcilable economic or ethnic conflicts, but rather from an expectation on one or both sides that gains for the rulers would outweigh their losses. Even allowing that the lives of thousands of subjects might often have been deemed a small loss, it is likely that many great or lesser wars would never have begun if the ruler of what was to be the losing side had assessed his resources more accurately. Also, Pyrrhus is probably not the only example of an all-too-costly victory; other victorious rulers may have discovered, through hindsight, that too high a price had been paid.

A second aspect of misperceiving the adversary is the failure to recognize similarities of interests and values, and the exaggeration and distortion of differences. These differences, moreover, are heavily loaded on the evaluative factor of Osgood, Suci, and Tannenbaum (1957): when our country is pitted against another, we readily accept that "we are strong, they are brutal; we are brave, they are stubborn; we are intelligent, they are sly." In this fashion, objectively similar attributes are given slanted connotations. Whatever differences really do exist, such as skin coloration or language, are also embodied with ethical significance: round, blue eyes are honest and fearless; slanted Oriental eyes bespeak of murderous guile and inscrutable, presumably craven, purpose. (Here, an interesting variant arises when one Oriental group is the enemy, while another is an ally. Subtle cognitive acrobatics are required in that case.)

For instance, White (1965) reports that American visitors in the U.S.S.R. usually meet with little understanding from Russians who are otherwise sympathetic to Americans when they try to explain the American defensive posture. Even those Russians who do not blindly accept Soviet party propaganda in its entirety, apparently are sincerely convinced of the wholly peaceable intent of their regime, and ascribe threatening intentions to the U.S. Government. The average Russian has surprisingly warm feelings toward America and the individual American (more so, we might venture to speculate, than is the case for the average American toward Russia and Russians). But there is also general puzzlement and resentment at American bases surrounding Russian territory, U-2 overflights, and, above all, the alliance with West Germany. There is, in other words, a different "reality" by which the two peoples live.

White is careful to point out that there exists a striking lack of objectivity in the Russian's perception. For instance, the Russian seems to be unaware that the United States had a monopoly on nuclear weapons for several years after World War II, and could have meted out terrible punishment to the Soviet Union at relatively little cost had its intentions been as aggressive as they are perceived.

We should be ill advised if we ascribed all views differing from the official U.S. viewpoint to paranoid delusions or consummate perfidy.

We cannot ignore that people respond not only to simple perceptual stimuli, but also to complex stimulus configurations, in terms of previous emotional and cognitive learning. Bronfenbrenner (1961) quotes the words of a Russian who justified his anger over the U-2 overflights by explaining how the response of the average American to seeing an airplane differs from that of the average Russian. To the American, the plane connotes leisure and adventure; to the Russian, it is a terrible reminder of devastations inflicted by the Luftwaffe.

We have here, then, a particularly tragic instance of a bidirectional self-fulfilling prophecy. The members of one nation, perceiving themselves, and their nation, as peaceful, view with alarm the ostensibly aggressive acts of the other. To arm against such threat seems to be not only permissible, but also a responsibility toward the defenseless, peaceloving peoples of the world. The other nation and its citizens may engage in nearly identical interpretations of the observed acts of the opponent, and respond in similar fashion. The question of who "started it all" is usually impossible of being answered objectively, for the answer to this question too depends upon the interpretation of a given act, which may be perceived as quite innocent by the perpetrator, but is seen as fraught with evil intentions by the other side.

Moreover, the contest is not likely to remain confined to a given level of intensity. The "need" for escalating one's own "defensive" weapons so as to deter the "threatening" adversary follows as an obvious corollary from the initial posture of mutual distrust.

Distorted perceptions seldom have a chance to be corrected, for conflict between parties usually cuts down communication between them. This may happen because the respective governments take steps to insure that their peoples are not "contaminated" by the "lies" of the other side. But even where such a communication breakdown is not imposed, Festinger's (1957) theory of cognitive dissonance indicates that people will actually show a preference for views that are not upsetting in being too divergent from their own (which are likely to have been formed by their mass media).

Any action taken by the other side is, in and of itself, suspect. Indeed, if the adversary were to undertake a sequence of behaviors exactly like those demanded by the other side (short of total capitulation or mass suicide), some unfathomable trick would be inferred. Psychological aspects of misperception of the other party's qualities and intentions, as well as of miscalculations of costs and gains, are therefore highly relevant. Strategy games and contrived bargaining situations (Rapoport & Chammah, 1965; Siegel, 1960; Siegel & Fouraker, 1960) have contributed much to our understanding of individual behavior in two-person conflicts. Perhaps the most important and consistent finding of these studies is that, in the long run, the effects of constricting aspects of a situation completely overshadow those or personality differences of the contenders which may have initially been present. People, it seems, do indeed become prisoners of circumstances.

Newcomb (1947) points out that the development of intergroup hostility often results in a breaking-off of contacts between the groups, thus allowing the misperceptions and hostilities to crystallize and become legitimized by tradition. These speculations were borne out in an experimental situation by Thibaut and Coules (1952). Simply cutting off communication between two individuals after hostility had arisen caused that hostility to increase further. While it would be hasty to infer that the obvious countermeasure of increasing contacts between conflicting groups always produces the desired effects of reduced antagonism, the policy of cutting off the sources of information not only has the originally intended effect of excluding hostile propaganda; it also eliminates the process of mutual familiarization.

The cutting off of communication does not automatically imply an increase in antagonism; people in communication with each other sometimes discover real conflicts of interest whose existence they had not expected. But in a situation where existing conflicts, whatever their merit, have *already* been overemphasized by the mass media in order to justify the conflicts, the interruption of communication may aggravate this antagonism in at least two ways. First, as hypothesized by Newcomb, an incubation process may take place, in which the members of one group remind themselves and each other of the other group's perfidy; their memory is generally aided by the mass media's unremitting campaign of innuendo and overt aggressiveness. In addition, no opportunity exists for acquainting onself with the other group's viewpoint. Granted that the other side would slant the presentation of the conflict in its own favor, a more balanced picture might nevertheless result than if only one biased position is known.

A third psychological source of intergroup conflict is the personality of its leaders. Even a republic or a democracy is not exempt from the whims and delusions of its leaders. Today, no less than centuries ago, invasions, suppressions, and wars have been precipitated by individuals in positions of power, not because their peoples' vital interests were at stake, but because some "personal insult" had to be avenged or because a personal gospel, not necessarily pertaining to one of the traditional faiths, required the conversion of the infidels. Harold Lasswell's *Psychopathology and Politics* (1930) deals with such personages. It is the author's contention that their incidence among political leaders may be greater than is commonly thought. We may regard his evidence with caution, but it would be extremely difficult—and unrealistic—to dismiss it altogether, and perhaps even to regard high political figures as exempt from human emotions and motives. Given that premise, the added minor premise that the leader has great power to act in accordance with those emotions and motives leads to a frightening conclusion.

Clearly, then, an understanding of emotion, motivation, and responses under stress on the one hand, and on the other, possible personality attributes related to the acquisition and maintenance of power are urgently needed.

Fourth, we have only the most superficial anecdotal information of the effects of such extreme stress as is represented by war or other catastrophes upon various aspects of individual and social functioning. More work is clearly needed, although one cannot help hoping that we may be spared both the opportunity and the need for such studies. Conceivably, the calculations, which some strategists have recently made popular, about how the United States would recover after nuclear conflict within a few years are based upon erroneous psychological premises.

Fifth, what are the processes whereby people can be persuaded to hate passionately the members of a group that only recently was warmly regarded? This question ties in closely with the preceding chapter, and is mentioned here only as an additional argument for the involvement of psychology in the study of international conflict. For instance, the notion that hatred for the outsider cements attachments within the group is not a new one. It is a frequent policy for a national government to depict the adversary in satanic or beastly terms, not so much to generate aggressive tendencies directly conducive to a successful pursuit of the war—after all, few civilians are likely to find themselves in combat situations—but to engender strong feelings of solidarity within the nation. Such solidarity—or, in Festinger, Schachter, and Back's (1950) term, "cohesiveness," would then manifest itself in greater effort in production, in more mutual help, and in greater endurance of the hardships of war, which are seen to be shared by others who have become emotionally close and important.

Finally, a greater understanding of psychological processes involved in the evaluation and resolution of real, and serious, conflict situations might point the way to acceptable alternatives to open conflict.

We have not really explored such situations in terms of cognitive, dispassionate problem-solving. Some aspects of this problem will be examined in Chapter XI.

We shall sum up, therefore, by strongly supporting the position that psychology has substantial contributions to make toward the understanding and control of international conflict, although the notion that such conflicts can be fully explained in psychological terms is rejected with equal vigor.

IX

Socially Beneficial Values and Behaviors

This chapter examines the applicability of the social learning approach to the acquisition of values and norms favoring cooperative and altruistic conduct. Altruism and cooperation exist even among the most primitive societies. The moral development of the child occurs through several stages. What are the norms relevant to altruism? How children learn about cooperation. What are the contributions of personality differences? A look at the vexing problem of noncorrespondences between values and behaviors.

WE SHALL NOW EXAMINE some of the real-life and experimental evidence in order to determine, first of all, whether cooperative and altruistic behaviors belong to a class of behaviors which are less "primitive" than aggression, and which, therefore, occur only at a higher phylo- or ontogenetic stage, or whether such behaviors depend for their acquisition and performance upon analogous processes as aggression; that is, whether not only altruistic behavior, but the totality of attitudes, beliefs, and values relating to such behavior can be usefully ascribed to social learning.

The argument whether cooperation or aggression "came first" in evolutionary development is largely a question of observer bias. Lorenz, for example, would have had little difficulty in expanding observations of altruism (and even self-sacrifice for other members of the species) in animals into as imposing a work as his book *On Aggression* (1963) (see also Hebb, 1966, pp. 247 ff.). It is not hard to see that instincts of this kind are indispensable equipment for the evolutionary viability of a species.

It has long been known that there exists no society "primitive" enough to lack norms that could be termed "altruistic." The individual learns early in life that he has binding responsibilities toward his family, although the definition of "family" may vary, and some relatives may be specifically excluded. In addition, a member of a society—or tribe— may acquire a sense of obligation or commitment toward the other members of the society; in larger societies, this attitude is usually latent, and is often superseded by intense antagonism arising from economic, familial, or status conflict. Yet even a large, "alienated" society, during periods of national crisis, often displays gestures of solidarity of which its own members may have deemed it incapable.

It has been the central argument of this book that interpersonal behaviors, including those that are expected to result in harm or benefit to another person, are preponderantly the result of social learning processes of varying degrees of complexity. We have not maintained that an organism had to learn *how* to be emotionally aroused; only what meaning to attach to such arousal, and the possible implications of such arousal for behavior. Here, as in our examination of the acquisition of aggressive values, tendencies, and behaviors, it might be of value to study not only the characteristics belonging to a cooperative or altruistic person but also to individuals who tend to elicit such behaviors, and, above all, situational determinants favoring them.

Again, it is almost a truism to assert that individuals accumulate specific experiences as well as cultural norms regarding the appropriateness of cooperative or altruistic acts. From the studies of Piaget (1932) we obtain impressive evidence that children develop through several stages of moral sophistication—from the simplest, represented by an unquestioning acceptance of rules as representing the natural order of things, to a well-formed conscience requiring no external monitor. There has been some disagreement with Piaget regarding his assertion that the developmental stages are invariant across individuals and cultures; but the essence of his work—that individuals, over time, develop a "value system" or conscience of increasing sophistication—can hardly be disputed. Society relies for its functioning not only on the establishment but also on the persistence of certain behaviors in the absence of frequent reinforcements. Without such a value system, the adherence to several norms would in each instance depend, not only upon a person's reinforcement history, but also upon narrowly defined stimulus cues.

Socially responsible attitudes and behaviors can be usefully divided into two categories: that of avoiding forbidden acts, and that of engaging in desirable, but not compulsory, behaviors. This distinction is also recognized by the Christian tradition, which speaks of sins of commission and sins of omission, by the law, which usually punishes the former more severely than the latter, and by informal social norms. For instance, a possibly needy person who commits theft incurs great opprobrium, as well as legal penalty. Another person, who fails to extend charity even though quite wealthy, but who has not broken the law, may not be universally beloved, but society tends to judge him with more leniency than it shows toward the person who has committed a theft.

Intentionally or otherwise, this division of normative attitudes and behaviors has been largely maintained by psychological investigators. One trend has sought to establish how the developing individual learns the "taboos" in his society; another has examined the formation of such "higher" values as cooperativeness, consideration, and altruism.

NORMS DEALING WITH TRANSGRESSIONS

The outstanding studies in the area of norms dealing with transgressions have been by Aronfreed and his associates. According to Aronfreed (1967), what acts are forbidden is learned initially through punishment which usually assumes the form of mild physical pain (such as a slap on the hand), paired with the parent's verbalization of disapproval.

In a subsequent, similar situation the child will experience (classically conditioned) fear, which may induce him to refrain from the forbidden act. However, the drive activating that behavior may overcome the avoidance drive engendered by the anticipation of punishment. It may also be the case that the child has not yet learned to abstract exactly what he had done wrong, especially if ostensibly similar situations sometimes have produced no punishment. Thus, taking cookies from the cookie jar may lead to reward without punishment at four o'clock in the afternoon, but not at five, when it is almost dinner time, and Mother does not wish Junior to spoil his appetite.

When faced with such an "ambiguous" stimulus situation, we may then observe various behaviors: the child may hesitate, and may become more agitated as he approaches consummation of the forbidden act, as would be predicted from Miller's approach-avoidance model. If the act is completed, we may continue to observe increased agitation. Aronfreed explains this as resulting from the expected approach of unavoidable punishment. On occasion we may observe the child attempting to terminate his fear by imitating the punishing behavior of the external agent by slapping himself on the wrist, perhaps accompanying the slap with such a remark as "Bad boy."

The behavioral control predicted by this model is therefore highly stimulus specific, and a slight change in the stimulus configuration may reinstate the behavior, while leaving subsequent anxiety present, indicating that proper abstraction of "guiding principles" has not yet taken place. Not having as yet learned the principle underlying the "taboo," such a physically slightly altered stimulus may lower the control enough to allow the behavior to recur, but at the same time retains enough of the original qualities to evoke anxiety, especially after the behavior has occurred.

At a later stage, where internalization utilizes symbolic processes to a greater degree, we would expect less stimulus and greater internal control and, in particular, a lesser incidence of punished or taboo behaviors evoked by stimulus situations that have some physical similarity to the original.

MAINTENANCE OF "TABOOS"

The question of how such norms, once acquired, maintain their strength over long periods without further reinforcement has caused some difficulty. Aronfreed (1967) proposes that even in situations involving supposedly long-term internalization, rewards may not be as infrequent as all that, since subtle indicators of social approval or disapproval may be present. This position, however, does not make clear how one social group, but not another, maintains its reinforcing properties; clearly, such approval could not originate from just any source, but would have to be highly specific.

In a way it is puzzling that such processes are sought, with the implication that once an attitude has been internalized, or a liking acquired, a person has to receive frequent periodic boosters or reinforcements to maintain the acquired attitudes.

We have confidence in the power of mediational processes to bridge long intervals of nonreinforcement. There is ample evidence that individuals, after years of intense deprivation, can reevoke both the taste and the desirability of a juicy steak, or the attributes of an attractive girl. The affective investment in one's "moral posture" at a time of crisis may be equally high, if not higher. A person confronted with a moral choice may be experiencing intensely the values he has internalized, possibly via identification, many years ago, and thus reevoke from a seemingly forgotten past the "right" choice. Even if the choice should go against those values, and conceivably encounter social approval, his postdecision guilt may be considerable. Such guilt, and the anxiety preceding it, would also explain why next time the person might not transgress again.

THE GENERATION OF ALTRUISTIC VALUES AND BEHAVIORS

Kohlberg (1963) has shown in considerable detail how children at various ages verbalize the moral implications and consequences of a number of hypothetical situations, including difficult moral choices. He describes six stages, ranging from a simple fear of punishment to an eloquently stated awareness of man's obligation to his fellowman. He also implies that moral standards stressing reciprocity such as "you scratch my back and I scratch yours" can really be seen as cases of arrested moral development; the ultimate stage involves no such mercenary considerations. We must note, however, that even Kohlberg's complex moral dilemmas do not allow for other determinants that may affect behavior in a situation. His situations involve the very important and basic question of what acts are considered as appropriate in a hypothetical situation. As we shall see, however, behavior does not always correspond to such values or attitudes, even where they are strongly held.

The basic conditioning processes (classical and instrumental) have been shown to be moderately effective in producing specific responses which could be broadly considered as altruistic. One class of responses, the sharing of resources, though often prompted by expectations of reciprocation, can sometimes be used to assess altruistic behavior in children who are too young to have developed abstract concepts of any complexity. One study on sharing behavior in children sought to determine whether primary or secondary reinforcers would be more effective in both learning and extinction. Fischer (1963) gave marbles to nursery-age children and then showed them a picture of a little boy (or girl) who did not have any marbles, asking them to donate some of their marbles to this less fortunate child. Children who were given bubble gum after sharing were more likely to repeat this behavior than children who were given verbal praise.

This finding is discouraging at first sight, since it is clearly desirable that children learn to behave altruistically for other than mercenary reasons. It is also puzzling in that it runs counter to many observations showing the powerful effects of praise. However, there are some confounding aspects to this study, because the effectiveness of Fischer's secondary reinforcer is questionable. Parents initially talk to a baby in warm, loving tones when they feed him, cuddle, or rock him. In later years they often couple praise with rewards, or what adults consider bribes. In this fashion their words and intonations acquire secondary reinforcing properties. Fischer had had no previous relationship with these children, and it may well be that his praise did not "mean" anything to them, whereas bubble gum was important, regardless of the giver. Had he paired the words with the bubble gum initially, his praise might have been more effective in maintaining the sharing behavior. It could also be the case that the experimenter who in manner or speech more closely resembled the childrens' parents might have administered secondary reinforcement more effectively. Some support for this speculation is offered by Midlarsky and Bryan (1967), who conducted a study in order to determine whether "expressive cues" (verbal praise) become a reinforcer when paired with the subjects' "positive affect" (presumably produced by a hug the experimenter gave the child).

The training procedure consisted of the subject watching the experimenter pull one of two levers. One lever led to a red light; the other to the appearance of one M&M candy. Training to pull the light lever was carried out in 5 different ways. Some children (E-H condition) re-

:eived a hug (H) after the expressive cue (E) "Oh, good, I see the
ed light." Others received the hug before the expressive cue (H-E condi-
ion) or a hug only (H condition), or an expressive cue only (E condi-
ion), or no reaction at all (0 condition). On "performance" or test trials,
ialf of the children in each condition except the last were given an expres-
.ive cue as reinforcement for pulling the light lever, while the other half
vere given no cue of any kind. It was expected that the E-H group
vould be most responsive to the expressive cue, and therefore would
>e most likely to choose the light lever, since it alone had received the
raditional paradigm of conditioned stimulus (expressive cue) followed
>romptly by the unconditioned stimulus (the hug). The E-H group, in
ontrast, represents an instance of the notoriously ineffectual method of
>ackward conditioning (the US precedes the CS). However, subjects in
>oth the E-H and H-E conditions who were given expressive cues during
he test trials preferred the "light" lever over the candy lever. Also, these
ame groups were most likely to donate candy to "needy children whose
>arents could not afford to buy them any candy." Midlarsky and Bryan
:oncluded that although the expressive cues were reinforcing, this was
iot due to the experimental manipulation—that is, they were not a newly
leveloped form of secondary reinforcement. One tends to concur in that
udgment; children probably learn the meaning of praise early, although,
•f course, it may differ in form and emphasis.

It should be obvious that the more basic learning processes of classi-
al and instrumental conditioning are less likely to be effective in the
nduction of desired values and behaviors than in the elimination of unde-
irable ones. In the latter, an already existing behavior, or class of be-
iaviors, can be extinguished with relative ease by withholding reinforce-
nents; or, anxiety can be conditioned to the relevant stimulus situation
ind incipient "taboo" responses can be halted by inflicting punishment.
Vhere desirable values and behaviors not yet in a person's repertoire
re concerned, the problem is a quite different one. Although instrumental
nd operant conditioning is, of course, immensely successful in producing
oncrete, specific behaviors, these techniques are not very efficient where
.bstractions and generalizations are the desired result.

In Chapter V, I cited Bandura and Walters (1963) to the effect
hat the learning procedures outlined above are not necessarily the most
fficient ones possible in social situations, and that imitation or modeling
an be powerful tools of social learning. Rosenbaum (1956) approached
tudents in the university library, and asked them to take part in his
esearch. For one third of the students, he first approached a stooge (sit-
ng near the student) who agreed to the request; for one third of the
tudents, he first approached a stooge who declined to be a subject; for
he remaining one third, the student was the only person approached.
n this last group approximately half of the students agreed to participate

and half of them refused. However, almost all of the students in the other two groups followed the lead of the stooge. An approach testing mediational processes similar to those discussed as imitation learning in Chapter V is represented by a study by Aronfreed and Paskal (1965) who used three procedures to train children to sacrifice M&M candies in return for the experimenter's joyous response. Those children who were given a hug and a joyous response when observing the experimenter sacrificing candies, performed in a more generous manner than children who were given only a hug or only a joyous response. This differs from the usual secondary reinforcement procedure in that the child's own response did not produce the primary reinforcer during learning. The child must in some way make inferences from observed responses of the rewarding model unto himself, or in other words, he must "identify." At the same time, these studies illustrate that quantitative relationships were involved even in these complex symbolic processes.

A study by Rosenhan and White (1967) examined the effectiveness of types of models for the performance of an imitative response. Three conditions were used in the study. For two of the groups, a 5-minute conversation between the graduate student model and the child began the experiment. The model was either pleasant and encouraging (positive reinforcement condition) or unpleasant and critical (negative reinforcement condition). A third group was given no prior interaction with the model. For all three groups, a noncompetitive bowling game was played first by model and subject, and then by subject alone, the model having left the room. When rewarded with two 5-cent gift certificates, the model ostentatiously placed one of the certificates into a box labeled "Trenton Orphans' Fund" and displaying pictures of the supposed orphans. It was found that 90 percent of the children who gave in the model's absence also gave when the model was in the room. The overall effect of the three conditions was not significant; that is, it did not matter how the model had behaved toward the children.

Other experiments are described in the literature which show that a nurturant relationship with a model facilitates certain types of behaviors but is irrelevant for other types of behaviors. For instance, Bandura and Huston (1961) found that aggressive responses were imitated, regardless of the model's nurturance. It may well be, as Rosenhan and White suggest that aggression is learned so early by children that the model need not be nurturant in order to elicit it; the behavior is not novel and does not have to be learned. Instead, the effect of the model is what Bandura and Walters (1963) call a disinhibitory one. Only where the model serves to transmit a relatively novel behavior, or one that usually is superseded by others, does the model's nurturance (and presumably other positively valued qualities) determine imitation by the observer.

There are three important determinants of imitative response that unfortunately have not been investigated in studies of beneficial behaviors. One is the consequences to the model of his own responses. We already know that the model who is rewarded for deviant behavior induces more imitation than the model who is punished for deviant behavior (Walters, Leat, & Mezei, 1963). Presumably, the analogous experiment involving altruistic behavior has been neglected because of its seeming triviality. Surely, there is little interest in the induction of "altruistic" acts undertaken because the agent expects rewards for himself similar to those of the model. But if observers of a rewarded model imitate more than those of a nonrewarded or punished model, and if this difference endures over time, then it is probably not due to expectations of tangible reinforcement on the part of the subject, but to the additional social clue of having done "the right thing" provided to the observing subject when the model is rewarded. The second determinant includes various characteristics of the subject such as dependency, emotional arousal, and previous social isolation (Lewis & Richman, 1964). All of these seem to be facilitators of social influence. (However, the possible fallacy involved in generalizing from well-learned or neutral behaviors to "new" or unaccustomed ones has been indicated in the studies of nurturant models.

Finally, it is at least possible that even covert constraint toward helping behavior induces a resentment similar to Brehm's "reactance" (1966). The evidence is scant, but Skydell (unpublished manuscript) found that children who were routinely required to contribute to a weekly charity gave less in a different, unconstrained giving situation than did children from whom no weekly contribution was exacted. It is of course possible that the children were "making up" for the many times when they had given in the past. But everyday observation also suggests that a giver's resentment against a recipient is not an unheard-of response.

NORMS RELEVANT TO THE DEVELOPMENT OF ALTRUISTIC VALUES AND BEHAVIORS

We shall now look at some of the major social norms demanding some kind of concern for the other person. Three such norms are relevant: Social responsibility, reciprocity, and distributive justice.

Social Responsibility

The notion of a social responsibility norm has been developed by Berkowitz and a number of his colleagues. They have suggested that persons in our society think that they are expected to help others who are dependent on them. In their first experiment (Berkowitz & Daniels, 1963), subjects were told that they were taking part in a test of supervisory ability. They were to perform a task according to instructions from a peer supervisor. In one group (high dependency), supervisors could win a prize if the subjects performed well. In the other group (low dependency), the supervisor's chance to win the prize did not depend on the subject's performance. Subjects worked harder in the high dependence than in the low dependence condition. Berkowitz and Daniels were particularly impressed by the consideration that the subjects themselves had nothing to gain from this behavior.

Alternative explanations, such as intersex effects and the experimenter's ostensible awareness of S's performance, were eliminated by a subsequent study (Berkowitz, Klanderman, & Harris, 1964). Again, it appeared that subjects were concerned with their own ideas of how they should be acting, rather than with the experimenter's approval. In another study, Berkowitz and Connor (1966) found that the greater the dependence of another, the harder the subjects worked on his behalf (see also Berkowitz & Daniels, 1964).

But social responsibility does not usually extend to all of humanity. There may be certain categories of persons who are labeled in our society as "persons to be helped," regardless of the situation. Adams (1967) quotes studies (Reiss, 1962; Sussman, 1959) which found that the closer the kinship, the greater the likelihood of mutual help. Daniels and Berkowitz (1963) manipulated the amount of liking that S presumably felt for the other person by making the responses on a personality questionnaire by a dependent peer similar (high liking) or dissimilar (low liking) to those of the subject. Subjects in the high dependency, high liking group exerted the greatest amount of effort for their dependent peers.

It might also be surmised that not only across cultures, but even in certain subcultures within a society, different norms regarding man's responsibility toward his fellowman might obtain. Berkowitz and Friedman (1967) classified subjects as members of either the entrepreneurial middle class (fathers working for themselves, sales people, professionals), or the bureaucratic middle class, or the working class. He found that the latter two groups acted more in accordance with the social responsibility norm than those in the entrepreneurial middle class. Subjects in this last group showed a greater tendency to give only to the extent that they themselves had been helped earlier; that is, they behaved in accordance with a reciprocity norm described below.

Reciprocity

It was mentioned above that persons who have been helped tend to help others on subsequent occasions. Gouldner (1960) has suggested that groups stabilize because of a universal norm of reciprocity. A helps B, and thus induces B to help A. In many cases, the debt is an indeterminate one. B can never quite pay it back, and thus is forced to continue interaction with A. Goranson and Berkowitz (1966) cite this formulation in opposition to the strict economic notion based upon calculation of expected returns for one's acts. Reciprocity need not be limited to a person who benefited S or is expected to do so in the future. An extended notion of the concept allows that a person who has received, or expects to receive, certain benefices may feel that he has a debt to other individuals in direct proportion to their resemblance to the original benefactor. Goranson and Berkowitz (1966) tested this notion of "generalization of reciprocity." They used their basic "dependency" situation in which a "supervisor" is dependent upon S's performance to win a prize. S had previously been helped or refused help by the "supervisor" himself, or by another confederate. Subjects who had been helped worked harder for the person who had helped them than for another person, whereas subjects who had been refused help worked harder for another person than for the person who had refused help. Goranson and Berkowitz concluded that both social responsibility and reciprocity norms were operating. They found evidence for the first in questionnaire results, and in the considerable increase in productivity (over a practice period) in those groups for whom two different confederates were involved. They also emphasized that the reciprocity found by them should be considered as a moral, rather than an economic, exchange.

Greenglass (1967) also used "prior help" conditions, and manipulated similarity between the confederate who helped or did not help and the "supervisor" whom the subject was asked to help. According to the social responsibility norm, similarity should not affect the help given to the (dependent) supervisor. On the other hand, the reciprocity norm generates the prediction that the obligation, or lack of it, would generalize to a similar, but not to a dissimilar, supervisor. Results of the "prior help" condition supported the hypothesis of social responsibility: The similar and the dissimilar other were helped about equally. However, in the "refused help" condition, subjects showed diminished effort on behalf of similar, but not dissimilar, supervisors, thus supporting a "reciprocity" intepretation.

Zener and Kaufmann (1967) attempted to distinguish among social responsibility, reciprocity, and expectations of economic reward, as follows: They used four reward groups. Partners were simulated, and potential rewards were either money for both players, points for both players, or money for one and points for the other. When the subject was playing for points, there was more cooperation in the group in which the partner was playing for money than in the group in which the partner was playing for points. This was interpreted as social responsibility. However, when the subject played for money, the results appeared more amenable to an interpretation of either reciprocity, simple economic hedonism, or a combination thereof.

LIBRARY ST. MARY'S COLLEGE

Distributive Justice

Another explanation of the efficacy of prior help in leading to increased effort would be in terms of an economic model of human behavior. Both Thibaut and Kelley (1959) and Homans (1961) present such models. Homans describes the way people in a group compare their rewards and costs to one another in the interests of distributive justice. He predicts that if the costs of certain members are higher than the costs of other members, distributive justice requires that their rewards should be higher. Distributive justice could be considered as an explanation of the Berkowitz and Daniels (1964) result. The three persons (subject, confederate who helped or did not help, supervisor) were grouped for the purposes of the experiment. When the confederate increased the rewards of the subject by helping him, then the subject felt compelled to increase his cost by helping his supervisor.

A slightly different notion of justice might be considered as an explanation of the results of Darlington and Macker (1966). These investigators found that persons who were led to believe that they had harmed another person were more likely to agree to donate blood than persons who had not been led to believe that they had harmed another person. Justice here would indicate that, having increased the costs of another person, the subjects felt obliged to increase their own costs.

THE MEANING OF COOPERATION

The crucial role played by cooperation in man's social structure has not been realized as long as one would surmise. It is true that in some sense any writing that deals with a social structure, such as, for instance, Plato's *Republic,* examines man as a member of a social system in which he plays a well-defined part. In his *Leviathan,* Hobbes, too, views the political state as an amelioration of mans' condition: without the state the life of man would be "solitary, poor, nasty, brutish and short."

But it is important to distinguish these symbiotic relationships, entered under considerable constraint and severe cost to freedom, from a situation in which equal partners enter freely into an arrangement in which each deliberately fosters the efforts of the other so that all may ultimately prosper.

It is possible, even plausible, to argue that cooperative behavior does not fall into the category of "true" altruism, since one of its principal determinants is the expectation of similarly cooperative behaviors on the part of another. From what has been said earlier, in Chapters V, VI, VII, and VIII, and the present one, this objection is only partially valid.

First of all, psychological theories, such as Festinger's Cognitive Dissonance (1957) and Bem's Self-Perception (1967), would lead us to predict that even acts undertaken initially for another reason may eventuate in the development of values corresponding more closely to the behaviors. Secondly, we have impressive experimental evidence that purely 'utilitarian" cooperation on tasks can lead to a rearrangement of a person's most central values.

Deutsch (1962) and Deutsch and Krauss (1960; 1962) report on the formation of cooperative behavior and trust as a function of very specific task situations. Deutsch and Krauss (1960) devised a game in which subjects were to act as owners of rival trucking companies, both of which were taking trucks to specific destinations. Profits were based on the time it took to complete a trip; it was preferable, therefore, to take the shortest road. This road was available to, and could be blocked by, both companies, and thus it could be used only if cooperative agreements were made. Each company also had its own alternate route, which was longer than the common road, and thus less profitable. The authors' findings showed that relative power to affect (and be affected by) the other's actions, conditions of communication, and so on, had vastly different effects upon not only the formation of cooperative (or competitive) behavior but also upon the formation of trusting and trustworthy attitudes.

A series of studies by Breer and Locke (1965) corroborates Deutsch's ideas that not only expedient cooperation but a substantial restructuring of a person's value system can result from his experiences in situations where he perceives the usefulness of a cooperative orientation. Sherif et al. (1961) showed that antagonistic groups of boys, when placed in a condition where cooperation is naturally beneficial, radically changed their attitudes toward each other.

AVAILABILITY OF ALTERNATE RESPONSES

It may be belaboring the obvious to state that when only one response is available, that response must be made. The more responses available, either in the individual's repertoire or because of the open nature of the situation, the less chance there is that any one response will be made. The principle of alternate responses is an accepted one in child rearing. When Johnny hits Little Alfie, he is perhaps reprimanded, but Mother will also try to distract him. When Alfie nibbles at the railing of his playpen, he may be offered the alternative of a hygienic, chewable toy. Deutsch and Krauss (1960), in the situation described earlier, provided both, one, or neither of the players with means of "threatening" the other player(s) by allowing the player(s) to block the shorter road to the goal. They found that the "no threat" dyads made the most profit, and the bilateral threat dyads made the least. Here, the mere opportunity to behave antagonistically produced such behavior.

Shomer, Davis, and Kelley (1966) in a similar study included one group of subjects who were given no alternate routes. These subjects learned to cooperate even when threat was available to them. In that case, removing an alternate response (to cooperation) increased cooperation.

Thus both removal of a potential for threat and removal of opportunities to retaliate against such threat without damage to one's own interest appear to be effective in enhancing cooperation.

THE IMPORTANCE OF SITUATIONAL DETERMINANTS FOR THE OCCURRENCE OF COOPERATION

One might be tempted to hypothesize that personality differences are strongly related to cooperative behavior. It seems more than plausible that a person's trusting attitudes, his tendencies to take advantage of another's trust in him, and just general hostility or misanthropy should influence behavior in a two-person situation where each person's outcome depends in part upon the other's choices. Deutsch (1962) found this to be true to some degree, but a series of studies by Rapoport and Chammah (1965), using prisoner's dilemma games, showed that *prolonged* interaction between two individuals takes a course that depends almost exclusively upon situational factors, with personality differences carrying negligible weight.

It is easy to think of real-life analogues where there are strict contingencies for the behavior of two individuals, in the sense that each possible behavior carries clearly defined outcomes for each participant. After a few exchanges, behaviors are likely to fall into a fairly constant, even though not entirely predictable, rut. This is not to say that personal attributes are never relevant (see below). But sometimes their effect is outweighed by situations. People do become trapped by circumstances!

PERSONALITY DIFFERENCES IN ALTRUISTIC AND COOPERATIVE VALUES AND BEHAVIORS

It may be that regardless of situation or expectation of reinforcement, certain persons are more likely to give help than others.

A number of scales have attempted to correlate personality differences and cooperation in game situations. Deutsch (1960) found that persons with high scores on the F scale were less trusting and less trustworthy than persons with low scores. "Trusting behavior" referred to a cooperative choice on the first move, and "trustworthiness" to a cooperative choice following the partner's cooperative move. [The F scale is a

"Potential for Fascism" scale, and includes such characteristics as rigid values, submission to authority, condemnation of those with other values, opposition to the subjective, power and toughness, generalized hostility, and belief that the world is a dangerous place (Brown, 1965)]. Other personality differences that have been investigated are flexible ethicality (Bixenstine, Potash, & Wilson, 1963), and Philosophies of Human Nature (Wrightsman, 1966).

Berkowitz and Daniels (1964), in a study outlined previously, measured the "social responsibility" of their subjects, using a portion of a scale developed by Harris (1947). Harris's scale is a self-report device that discriminated between elementary school children who had a reputation with their peers for acting in a socially responsible manner and those children who did not possess such a reputation. For instance, the items used by Berkowitz and Daniels included the following:

"It is always important to finish anything that you have started."
"It is of no use worrying about current events of public affairs; I can't do anything about them anyway."
"In school my behavior has gotten me into trouble."

In the first statement, it is more socially responsible to agree. In the last two statements, it is more socially responsible to disagree. It was found that in the prior help, high dependency condition, subjects who expended more effort for the supervisor had higher marks on the social responsibility scale (r = + 40). Stone (1965a,b) pointed out that the items were not subtle ones, and that perhaps the scale measures only a tendency to present oneself in a favorable light. In support of this, he found that social desirability scales correlated positively (.65 for the Crowne-Marlowe [1964] scale and .53 for the Edwards [1957] scale) with the Berkowitz-Daniels (1964) scale. But, as Berkowitz (1965b) pointed out, these results were not surprising. The social desirability scales assume that the high scorer "knows what is socially proper and wants to appear proper." He cited an unpublished study of Berkowitz and Lutterman (1968) in which high and low scorers on the Social Responsibility scale were given interviews. The high scorers were more likely to contribute money to educational and religious organizations, to do volunteer work, to belong to several organizations, and to be more conventional in such matters as religious beliefs. In other words, one (very useful) aspect of social desirability may consist of *knowing* what is the appropriate behavior for a given situation. In addition, those much maligned determinants of behavior, Social Desirability (Edwards, 1957) and the Approval Motive (Crowne & Marlowe, 1964), may not in themselves be reprehensible for yet another reason: granted that a total and enduring lack of inner values, with a corresponding alertness to situational demands, makes for a rather unattractive and unreliable personality, results of earlier-cited studies indicate that acts initially undertaken because they seemed to be the socially approved thing, and immediate social reinforcement was expected, may, after all, become internalized and become part of a person's value system.

NONCORRESPONDENCE BETWEEN VALUES AND BEHAVIORS

There has been some concern recently with the failure of law-abiding citizens to assume what could be called basic social responsibilities in crisis situations. In some well-known instances, a person who had seriously injured another had already left the scene, yet many people either passed by the victim, or even stood around staring at him, without either helping directly or calling for help (Milgram, 1963; Kaufmann, 1968; Darley & Latané, 1966; Latané & Darley, 1967).

It should be kept in mind that we are not speaking of the "transgressions" of those who simply hold values quite different from our own, and act in accordance with them. Our concern is with instances of, say, cheating by children (Hartshorne & May, 1928; Brogden, 1940) and, more tragically, destructive obedience (Milgram, 1963) or nonintervention by bystanders in crisis situations (Kaufmann, 1968), even though the populations under consideration had both responsible values and beliefs in their own propensity for acting in accordance with them.

Darley and Latané (1967) view this particularly distressing phenomenon as a diffusion of responsibility: the more the people who witness a crisis situation, the less likely it is that a particular person will intervene, or that any help will be forthcoming at all. Experimental results impressively support their hypothesis. But Kaufmann (1968) found nonintervention even with a single witness. In any event, these findings still do not tell us why so large a proportion of our population, singly or in a gathering, show such a low *absolute* level of concern. We shall attempt no uncorroborated speculation here about practices in other countries. It is also not entirely legitimate to point to the early pioneer, or, say, present-day Amish settlements, and ascribe their greater concern for one another to a "sounder moral fiber." Both instances deal with groups where interpersonal acquaintance, even friendship, encompasses almost all members, whereas our examples deal with individuals who have no previous acquaintance. Yet one wonders, legitimately, why behavior in a crisis situation is sometimes found to deviate from quite sincerely professed values. Our attempt to understand this occasional discrepancy between values and behaviors, specifically where "noble thoughts" and less noble acts are concerned, might have to take into account a basic difference that distinguishes the learning of altruistic values from exploitative or aggressive ones, even though the processes of such learning are presumed to be analogous.

Contrary to aggression, altruism cannot generally be reinforced by tangible reward. An aggressive act that forces another child to relinquish a coveted toy, reinforces the aggressive behavior and increases the strength of a habit of committing "instrumental aggression." But since "instrumental altruism" is a contradiction in terms, such reinforcement is not generally appropriate where an altruistic act has occurred.

In addition, altruistic behavior is also more rarely rewarded, especially by peers. One is tempted to speculate about the response of even most adults to, say, a child's altruistic response. The author has only casual observations to support these speculations, but apparently the prevalent response toward the child is not one of delighted commendation, but of suspicion. "He must be after something," or "I wonder what he did wrong," might be a more frequent response to attempts at altruism than we care to admit.

Children acquire what we need not hesitate to call a "conscience" (Piaget, 1932; Aronfreed, 1967; Kohlberg, 1964). They learn by direct tuition that certain values are desirable, and others are not. But they also learn to make inferences from the behavioral outcomes of others, as well as their own. For instance, if a child observes that selfish behavior pays off, he need not be told that "selfishness is a noble value" in order to internalize its desirability. Should he receive admonitions contrary to his own experience, to the effect that selfishness is to be shunned, he may very well internalize a quite different value, namely "maintain that selfishness is undesirable," but his behavior could then hardly be expected to be unselfish! The process of self-observation and inference in the formation of values may be the basis for the relative congruence of aggressive values and aggressive behaviors, as opposed to the frequent discrepancy between moral, including altruistic, values and behaviors. Let us take the example of an aggressive value and an altruistic one. The former may be learned frequently through the inferential, self-observational process we have just described, even though direct transmission or identification-produced internalization is relatively rare, since our mores do not favor preaching the *homo homini lupus* doctrine (Chapter II). We observe others, and ourselves, benefiting from various kinds of selfish or aggressive behaviors, and make appropriate inferences from these observations. There are good grounds, therefore, to develop a value system quite congruent with behaviors and outcomes with which one has experience.

The situation with regard to moral, socially responsible and altruistic values is quite different. Here, there is a considerable impact of direct tuition. Commandments, urgings, and intimations abound as to what our duties are. Unfortunately, observation of self and others indicates that behaviors very different from the advocated ones frequently are rewarded.

Not only would we expect observers to imitate behaviors that pay off rather than behaviors that have been recommended to them as praiseworthy (Rosenhan & White, 1967), but even where a close identification with the socializing agent exists, one would expect at best two value systems to develop. One of these might be on the order of "Cheating is all right, if you don't get caught. Everybody does it, even the person I admire, who tells me that honesty is its own reward"; the other might be stated thus: "Always maintain that cheating is dishonest and contemptible." If we observe these two statements carefully, we can see that they contain, especially for a child, no real contradiction. One favors cheating when useful and safe, the other advocates the utterance of certain statements. Not only is there no intimation that value system number two should be supported by honest behavior, but the acquisition of the two value systems may actually lead to the inference of a corollary, to the effect: "It is all right to say one thing and do another," a value paraphrased not infrequently in our culture by the noble dictum "Don't do as I do, do as I say," or, as more elegantly put by Oscar Wilde, "Hypocrisy is Vice's Concession to Virtue."

The educational philosophy of permissiveness of 30 years ago seems to have penetrated many of our adult values today. Transgression is usually viewed as calling for indulgence in conjunction with self-examination by the nontransgressors, with the implied suggestion that "we are all guilty," and that therefore no special blame should attach to the actual offender. Although such an approach has its definite purpose, particularly with regard to the self-righteous, vindictive authoritarian, it fails to provide any motive to past or prospective transgressors for behaving in a socially responsible fashion. Not only philosophers and social critics, but psychologists too have questioned the validity of this approach for the welfare of Society (Mowrer, 1967; Keniston, 1965). Indeed, it is easy to see that such a state of affairs affords little opportunity to practice socially responsible behaviors. More important, it may *preclude* the learning of appropriate values, both because suitable models and norms are lacking, and because the individual has no way of observing relevant behaviors of his own from which to infer his value system.

In conclusion, our analysis of altruistic behaviors and values in terms of a social learning context implies that in all likelihood it is as unprofitable to look for the "purely" altruistic or cooperative act as for the absolutely evil one. This does not of course imply that values are meaningless; on the contrary. It is a corollary of the basic premise of this volume that not only specific behavioral dispositions but even the highest values are at least indirectly the result of individual experiences. But an approach, in order to be useful, must view even these values as quantitative rather than as all-or-none qualities, as well as take account of other determinants for a given act.

X

A Meaningful Definition of "Attitude," and a Model for Aggressive and Altruistic Behaviors[1]

Here, we first attempt to define "attitude" in such a manner as to make the term *relevant* for behavioral choice.

A formal model is then introduced, which attempts to predict behaviors from attitudes, the utilities of outcomes expected to result from the various possible behaviors, and existing habits of reponding to certain stimulus situations in given ways.

WE SHALL NOW CONSIDER how it might be possible to design a model for the two contrasting aspects of interpersonal behavior—aggression and altruistic acts—which would permit us to predict with some accuracy what type of behavior will occur, given a person's "habitual" predisposition, the focus or target person of his potential act, and the environment, especially the social environment, in which the act would take place.

THE MEANING OF VALUES AND ATTITUDES FOR BEHAVIORS

The question of attitudes or values has remained dormant during our examination of aggressive behaviors. It is true that notions such as "aggressive habits," "identification," and "internalization" imply an underlying cognitive structure. But in our discussion of aggression we could

[1] A theoretical paper by the author examining sources of attitude-behavior discrepancies is in preparation.

115

afford to treat such submerged or hypothetical events lightly; we had no reason to consider any discrepancies between such inner states, however inferred or assessed, and behaviors. Our concern was to minimize *both* the nonvisible tendencies and the overt acts. Although attitude-behavior discrepancy is theoretically symmetrical in that it can refer to "bad" values and "good" behavior as well as vice versa, our concern is usually with the discrepancy between a desirable value and the deplorable human imperfection which makes the person stoutly affirming this value deviate from it in practice. Therefore, the problem becomes salient when we deal with desirable attitudes or values which, alas, are not translated into appropriate behaviors.

While we may spare no effort to ensure that a person does not acquire antisocial or destructive values, we dwell lightly upon the case of a person holding a harmful attitude, but acting beneficially. The noncorrespondence between attitudes and behavior is not always distressing; the occasional gesture of mercy on the part of a habitual criminal, or forbearance shown by a usually cold and unforgiving individual, are cases in point. But we are rightly concerned when our strategy of encouraging the acquisition of altruistic and socially responsible values fails to result in corresponding behaviors.

Our interest in the relationships between what we might call dispositions or attitudes and behavior derives from more than a narrow interest in people's noble motives and less-than-noble deeds. The topic is more general, and applies to any behavior in which what we might call by the shorthand term "moral issues" are relevant. For the purposes of this volume, however, we shall examine only those attitudes and behaviors that we have chosen to call "interpersonal effectance."

The concept of "interpersonal effectance" includes those behaviors undertaken by one person with an expectation (greater than zero) of harming or benefiting another person. It should be noted that, as before, the variable "expectation" is preferred to "intent," not so much because "intent" as an intervening variable is more refractory to being related to observable antecedents and consequents, as because it is a quantitative rather than a qualitative concept. "Intent" is either present or absent, but "expectation" allows for instances where a favorable or unfavorable outcome for another person has some subjective probability of occurring, though possibly only as a "side effect" of an act having a principal goal of another nature. The notion of interpersonal effectance, therefore, does not imply that the impact of one person's act upon another is the only, or even the major, goal of that act. Applicability of the concept requires only that (1) another person be involved in the event; and (2) the actor's subjective probability of altering the total well-being of the other be greater than zero. Thus "aggressive behaviors" as defined in Chapter I constitute one subset of the class of interpersonal behaviors we have defined as "effectance," while altruistic behaviors are another. Information or persuasion, that is, the attempt to provide another person with new knowledge, could be considered another such class.

Our task, then, is to establish what we mean by a "value," or more specifically, an attitude related to the well-being of another person and to establish possible grounds for hypothesizing a relationship between such attitudes and the behaviors we have defined as interpersonal effectance.

We more or less tacitly assume that our society aims at fostering and maintaining in its members a system of values or norms which are prosocial and altruistic in nature. This, of course, is a major aspect of socialization, and, as we have said in the preceding chapter, the purpose of such a system is not only to restrain a person from committing specific misdeeds, and to induce him to perform specific acts in particular situations, but also to acquire a general value system, or a "conscience," which will serve as a guide and monitor in new or unusual situations. A fully developed social conscience implies a system of generalized or generalizable rules. But even the possession of such a system does not necessarily eliminate the problem that behaviors are not necessarily highly correlated with such rules.

The psychological literature is bedeviled by a persistent lack of correspondence between values and attitudes on the one hand and behavior on the other. The state of the world being what it is, it is more frequently the case that people have noble values, and sometimes even fine intentions, which remain unmatched by corresponding behaviors; but it is not unheard of that a person had started out with intentions he knew to be craven, only to find at the moment of having to make a behavioral choice that his "better nature" prevailed.

If we make the effort to look at the topic dispassionately, we find that such discrepancies do not happen quite so often as one would think. It happens that psychological investigations concerning them have dealt with what might be called "conflict," or better, "crisis" situations. There is little reason to believe that a person who states that he prefers pistachio ice cream will not order it more frequently than any other, and will also predict his own behavior with reasonable accuracy. Excepting, chiefly, in cases of extreme coercion (and temptation), people are not as inconsistent as all that. We do not get excited over the fact that a person who likes both pistachio and vanilla may choose one over the other. Our concern, which I state with deliberate vagueness at this point, is why people often do *not* act in correspondence with their stated beliefs or values. The frequent noncorrespondence between what people say and what they do has produced considerable distrust of attitudes as useful predictors of behavior. Some alternative solutions have been proposed, such as "Let us disregard attitudes entirely." Or, "Let us ask people what they *would* do, if it is impossible to observe them actually doing it." But sometimes people are asked to *predict* their own behavior, and even then they are far off the mark.

The point has also been made that because *statements* of (alleged) attitudes and physical acts are really two kinds of behavior, no correspondence should be expected. This argument cautions us on a very important point. Many of our so-called attitudes are indeed statements that have *no* referent to specific behaviors in given situations. To say "I am a liberal" supposedly denotes not a party affiliation (since "liberal" is not spelled with a capital), but a constellation of attitudes and beliefs properly called a "value." If on a given occasion the speaker were to act in an "illiberal" fashion—for instance, by refusing to sell his home to a Negro—two paths are seemingly available to the psychologist: (1) He can ignore the person's alleged political and social feelings and concentrate upon the determinants of his discriminatory act; or (2) he may, quite independently, seek the specific correlates of his generally liberal posture and *their* determinants, but regard such attitude statements as unrelated to behavior; there exists for him no problem of inconsistency or conflict. Another psychologist, who is not yet entirely convinced that cognitive processes are nonexistent, or at best irrelevant, will be puzzled by the "inconsistency" between the person's value system and statements of belief and his specific act of discrimination. Eventually, one or the other will in all likelihood be ascribed to "social desirability" or "conformity."

The importance of such situational determinants is, of course, enormous and undeniable; the existence of these factors can give us additional information about situations and individuals. But if we were to dismiss altogether attitudes as contributors to behavior, it might be selling short our goals. Also, a consideration of attitudes does not automatically imply a resorting to some of the lamentable devices that have masqueraded in the literature as measures of man's "true" inner state. First of all, the present imperfection of a measuring device does not invalidate the usefulness of a concept, as long as some progress toward greater accuracy may eventually be expected. Secondly, as Jones and Davis (1965) have shown, behaviors can serve as clues to underlying attitudes (and what they call "dispositions"), particularly when those behaviors are not obviously situation-dictated or normative. But if attitudes are to have any usefulness for behavioral prediction, we must first of all ensure that the attitudes measured refer to situations where a behavioral choice is relevant, instead of representing noble-sounding, but quite generic and content-free, statements of faith.

It has often been held that an attitude consists of three presumably independent components—namely affect, cognition, and conation—and that a given attitude may be composed of different amounts of each of these components (Krech, Crutchfield, & Ballachey, 1959). Thus, a certain attitude could have a negligible conative or behavioral component. Apparently this means that a person could have positive or negative feelings and beliefs about something, without having any intention or expectation of doing anything about it. Clearly, if the person is then observed in a behavior that is related to that attitude, it should not surprise us if there is little correspondence between the "attitude" and the ostensibly related behavior. However, the present definition differs radically. As the term is used here, "attitude" refers to a (possibly implicit) behavioral predisposition *derived* or *inferred* from affective and cognitive elements. Without the behavioral readiness, those elements have no anchoring in reality, and it is therefore meaningless to look for a relationship between them and an observed event. It might be asked whether it is not possible to have a favorable attitude toward, say, space exploration, without the slightest expectations of being in any way involved in it. We would maintain that here, too, the "sentiment" becomes a "favorable attitude" only when it implies, at the very least, *assent* to certain events *favoring* the object of "space exploration" (such as "increased research"), and opposition to events unfavorable to the object.

Further, the affective and the cognitive "components" are not seen as functioning, as it were, side by side as coordinate and independent elements. Heider's (1946) work as well as that of Peak (1960) and of Rosenberg (1956) imply an interaction process that becomes activated when the elements and their referent become salient. The tendency toward consistency, called by various terms as "balance" or "congruence," makes the enduring disparity of, say, a strong affective and a weak belief component somewhat unlikely. Strong liking quickly becomes buttressed by strongly held favorable beliefs, and such beliefs conversely generate affective involvement.

The affective basis of an attitude may originate from classical conditioning. Thus a person whose visits to the bank have been associated with anxiety over economic problems may develop a negative emotional response to banks in general and, through mediating processes, to symbols related to finance. On the basis of consistency notions, we might then also expect him to accept items of information which reflect negatively upon the aversive object class, and to favor events which would impair its power and threat. Ultimately, given the opportunity to engage in, or at least to envisage engaging in, behaviors promising some such effect, he should, other things being equal, show greater tendencies to engage in these behaviors than in behaviors having different goals.

Take the example of a person being strongly opposed to sending American colonists to populate Mars. This sentiment may exist without relation to reality. Such a feeling, however, if made salient or brought before his attention would be quite meaningless, even to himself, unless he justified it by citing various *beliefs* (cognitions), veridical or otherwise, to the effect that such colonization would have what he considers undesirable consequences. This process, furthermore, is inseparable from a behavioral (*conative*), or better, an "outcome" component, whereby he would engage in, or at least favor the occurrence of, certain events that would reduce the likelihood of Mars becoming the 51st State of the Union, and, conversely, refrain from acts or oppose events that would make such an endstate more likely.

The interactions between strength of feelings, beliefs, and position toward events are also illustrated in the work of Rosenberg and Hovland (1960), Peak (1958), and Rosenberg (1956). When an opportunity for action on the person's part arises, then we should quite reasonably expect him to behave so as to bring about the outcomes he favors. This is not to say that other determinants do not enter into the picture; they are, as we shall see, indispensable in prediction of behavioral choices.

Despite laborious arguments to the contrary, this relationship is really not questioned in practice. Our whole socialization process, from the religious or secular education of the child to the development of moral integrity and social responsibility in the adult, depends upon it. Only rarely do we favor complete coercion or very strong response habits to induce desired behaviors. More frequently, we seek to *convince* that such behaviors are indeed desirable. In addition, even where compliance may be enforced at one point in time, it is often expected that the coerced individual will eventually experience a "change of heart; that is, that his attitude will correspond more closely to the act he has already committed. As Machiavelli observed, another person's likes or dislikes would be meaningless to us, unless we anticipated further acts on his part which would affect us. Having induced an attitude consonant with behaviors we favor, either by persuasion, or Festinger's (1957) postdecision dissonance, or according to Bem's (1967) theory, through self-perception, we perceive a greater "likelihood" than before that in the future, faced with a relevant situation, the person will behave in the desired fashion.

Thus, in all probability, no process of teaching, preaching, or discussion can be separated from such implicit behavioral consequences. Evidently, attitude can be overriden by, for instance, a strongly ingrained habitual or "automatic" response (a situation which clinically would be described as "fixation") or by immediate utilitarian or hedonistic considerations of hope or fear. We do not for a moment ignore the powerful effects of the situational pull or the demand characteristics of a situation. But instead of arguing that it is pointless to look for a correspondence, or even a relationship between attitudes and behaviors, it is suggested that "attitude" is, by definition, a component of behavior.

This "ideal" or "ought" behavior which the person may perceive as required by the situation may be the result of a direct instruction by someone else whose word is accepted without question, or more often, it may be deduced or inferred by the actor from his own value system.

Thus, the soldier may consider risking his life out of unquestioning obedience to a leader who is obeyed, not because of fear or hope of reward, but because the actor believes him to be "right," and to know best. On the other hand, the soldier may examine the situation and his values and beliefs, and arrive at the following syllogism:

> Worthy men do not hesitate to die for their country.
> I am a worthy man.
> Therefore, I should not hesitate to die for my country.

The behavior is the same, but the process is quite different. To repeat, the attitude is seen as an affectively charged set of beliefs, with inextricable implications for behavior. These implications may be deduced by the individual himself, or may require probes and clarifications by another person. Psychological counseling is one instance where one person helps another to find out "what he really wants to *do*" in order to implement his values. But the attitude is not the sole determinant of behavior, and despite the clarifications introduced above, factors other than attitudes may affect the ultimate act.

THE COMPONENTS OF INTERPERSONAL EFFECTANCE

Conditioned Response to the Stimulus

In some instances, a stimulus may elicit an affective response. We have argued insistently that such an autonomic, cognitively labeled, response—for example, "anger"—should not be confused with behaviors. However, we have also proposed that self-observed emotional state may serve as one clue in a person's classification of the stimulus, as well as an energizer of a response. In these two respects, then, it is a relevant component toward the ultimate behavioral outcome.

Most frequently, even these simple affective responses imply complex cognitive processes. It may be possible to condition classical and instrumental responses to unequivocal stimulus situations, say, that of a person suffering extreme and bloody injury. Indeed, from some animal studies one might even venture the speculation that an "empathic" response to another's extreme distress is "built in," and that human individual experience may produce an *unlearning* of that "built-in" response, as, for instance, when the mutilation of a despised enemy is calmly viewed. However, the emotional distress conditioned to the Japanese (but not to the Chinese) countenance a few years ago was obviously not due to the stimulus as such, but to complex, symbolically mediated associations to a stimulus, categorized not only in terms of its objectively discernible characteristics but also in terms of the cognitive labels of "evil" and "treachery" attached to it.

Classification of the Stimulus

One response that the individual usually makes when confronted with a stimulus situation consists in categorizing or classifying it. Clearly, such a classification can take place along innumerable dimensions, such as "edibility," "size," "usefulness as a weapon," "genuineness" (as opposed to "fake"), and so on. Despite its superficial similarity to the stimulus-bound response pattern of, say, one male stickleback fish at the sight of another (Tinbergen, 1953), a similarity which, as was asserted in Chapter II, led Lorenz to make his unwarranted generalizations, the present situation differs decisively. First of all, Chapters VI, VII, and IX, which discuss how a person learns to hate or feel warmly toward others, make it quite clear that the relevant generalization and discrimination processes involve quite complex symbolic processes, although simple perceptual ones may also be present. A stimulus may be classified as "Jewish" (and therefore, to a person who has learned to hate Jews, as "noxious") on the basis of such simple facial characteristics as the shape of the nose, but also because of complex inferences and deductions. based upon hearsay information. In either case, *both* the categorization and its reasons are learned. Emotion, while it may be present as a classically conditioned response, and thus may aid in the categorization of the stimulus by providing an additional clue, is not a necessary prerequisite, especially when the categorization of members of a given stimulus class has become habitual or established. However, the effect of emotional arousal at this point may be that of a probabilistic operator, which changes the likelihood that a stimulus will be classified in a certain way. An aroused (but not necessarily "angry") person may respond more rapidly, or consider fewer classification alternatives than he ordinarily would, and increase the likelihood of an aggressive response that would otherwise not occur. In general, arousal produces more "extreme" or affect-laden classifications, both favorable and unfavorable. As we have seen, then, this cognitive classification may, but need not, be influenced by a positive or negative emotional response. Also, it is worthy of note that, for instance, the proportion of stimulus situations classified as "noxious" could serve as an operational definition of a person's "hostility."

Both the conditioned response to the stimulus and its (not necessarily independent) cognitive and evaluative classification are, for our purposes, seen as determinants of the "pure" or "ought" predisposition, which we have called an "attitude," and which can be stated as "This is what a person (like me) should ideally do in such a situation." This further elaboration should also make it clear that our definition of such a "pure" or "ought" attitude carries no moralistic overtones. The question whether the attitude is noble or not is a separate one; what concerns us here is the assumption that the attitude can initiate at least a partial response that is not yet affected by considerations of utility or by strongly established response habits or "fixations," which may also determine which response is in fact completed.

Utility

The simplest and most obvious determinant of behavioral choice in a situation is, of course, utility. A driver approaching a stop sign has at least two alternatives available to him. He may stop, or he may ignore the sign. It is a reasonable conjecture that the perceived or suspected presence of a policeman will decisively affect the respective probabilities of the two (mutually exclusive) behaviors.

The calculus of utility has only recently found its way into psychological thinking (Siegel, 1960; Siegel & Fouraker, 1960; Edwards, 1954). Traditionally, it is defined as the algebraic sum of positive values of the outcome multiplied by their respective probabilities, minus negative values multiplied by respective probabilities. Edwards (1954) has argued cogently that values as well as probabilities should be measured subjectively rather than objectively. In situations involving complex moral choices, this is even more important. Such a reward as "public social approval," or the risk of "physical suffering," obviously can hardly be considered otherwise than in terms of the subjective valuations a person attaches to them.[1]

Habitual or "Fixated" Behaviors

In some instances, a person may respond to a stimulus with a strongly overlearned, habitual, or "fixated" response that occurs without evidence of behavioral choice. Such responses or "habits" constitute a good part of our daily behaviors. We "unthinkingly" button our shirts, open a door, remove our hats in an elevator. Quite often, in fact, our jobs and various social interactions, including those with our family and friends who are dear to us, consist of such "unthinking" behaviors or attitudes. We might call this syndrome "unthinking," or "automatic," behavior—and I wish to make no speculations here about subconscious motivations.[2] It is much simpler to hypothesize that overlearning has oc-

---

[1] A case has been made for another component of behavior, called "contagion" (Redl, 1949; Wheeler, 1966). It could be defined as a person's tendency to engage in behaviors that are neither habitual, nor utilitarian, nor—to himself—praiseworthy. Instead, he will perceive himself impelled to act in a certain way, possibly at some cost or risk to himself. Granted that such a resultant tendency toward "mob behavior" is relatively rare, it is nevertheless a valid component if we allow that even where it does not eventuate in actual behavior, it may play a part in the behavioral decision. For the sake of simplifying our model, however, we shall not consider this component.

[2] "Unthinking," or "automatic," behaviors need not be callous or selfish. A fireman routinely and "automatically" may engage in socially beneficial acts.

curred, in the sense that relatively few response alternatives have led to the early adoption of a response pattern, which is then performed and reinforced many times. The stimulus-response contingency, in other words, becomes relatively stable. The subjective probability that attaches to a response alternative may, in fact, be the principal difference between "consciously" evaluated alternatives, and "un-" and "pre-" conscious ones. A person may not consider an alternative because it has, for him, a very low probability of performance. This is distinguishable from the notion of "set," or from "not knowing about the alternative at all." Frequently, when we have a chance to *ask* people why their behavior in a crisis situation differs so widely from their ideals, and even from what they originally *thought* they would have done, we seldom hear the answer "Why, that never occurred to me at all." On the contrary, people seem quite aware of other response alternatives, but perceive a near-zero probability of engaging in them.

Even where a response is not wholly "automatic" or "fixated," response habit hierarchies are, not surprisingly, of extreme importance. "Having always done it this way" is, for better or for worse, a powerful predictor of future behavior.

BEHAVIOR AS A FUNCTION OF ATTITUDE AND THE OTHER COMPONENTS

We can see now why our hypothetical soldier's attitude toward his duty to his country does not automatically imply that heroic self-immolation will result. The actual behavior will be a function also of response habits and other considerations. Most human beings have strongly overlearned the habit to avoid dangerous situations, and the best-intentioned man may find himself turning his back on a frightening confrontation. More frequently, the unrewarding payoff functions of such a situation ("I have a probability x of gaining a medal, which has, at best, a moderate value, and a probability y of losing my life, which is very dear to me") may prevent even those who are fully convinced of the nobility of self-sacrifice to choose a more moderate, and safer, course. Finally, real or imagined situational demands toward bravery may not only reverse the scales once more in our example of the hesitant hero, but "make brave men out of cowards." (A "coward" in this instance could be not only a person with an irresistible aversive response to combat but also one whose well-organized attitudes call for anything but heroism.)

Many situations do not load on one or more of these components. Thus, beholding a dish of chicken and one of tuna, a person may have an immediate preference, possibly intensified by a classically conditioned affective response, such as pleasant anticipation at the thought of eating chicken, or a shudder produced by the reevocation of its slaughter. The utility of the respective choices may become relevant if there should be a difference in price. It is unlikely, though, that the choice will be considered in terms of which of the two dishes one should "ideally" choose. Or, a situation may have no utility in that the actor expects no rewards or punishments for choosing one behavior over another. Also, he has no pertinent habits or behavior preferences that have developed in the past. But he entertains very strong ideas as to what the "right" behavior in a situation is.

In sum, of the three components of the behavioral choice—response habit, situation-specific utility, and internalized norms—one or more may be present.

Having endured until now, the reader will, it is hoped, bear with us as we symbolize, in a simplified fashion, our description of interpersonal effectance, as follows:

$$\text{Pot. (Beh.}_{ijk}) = f \ (A_{ijk} + U_{ijk} + H_{ijk})$$

This means that the potential of behavior k in situation j, for individual i, is an additive function of the intrinsic or ideal attitude i holds toward that behavior, translatable as "This is what the type of person I am (or I should ideally wish to be), should do in this situation," plus the utility he expects to result from this behavior, plus the habit strength of the behavior. The equation is simplified in that it assumes that A is a resultant, or vector, of already resolved value conflicts, such as may arise, for instance, when an initiated aggressive response elicits unexpected aggression anxiety. In other words, it is assumed that the actor *knows* what he "ought" to do in this situation. Also, as explained earlier, that utility term should be understood as being composed by the value times probability sums, both positive and negative.

Now we come to the most important part of this discourse. Our everyday conversations contain descriptions such as "He acts in accordance with his beliefs—he is a man of principle"; as opposed to, perhaps, "He waters down his principles on the slightest provocation." What is being said, I suggest, is not that a given person passionately subscribes to a given attitude, but that, even though two individuals may hold a specific ideal preference with equal vigor, the behavioral decision of one person may be more highly influenced by his ideals than that of the other. This individual difference could be translated, in the case of a mildly held attitude, in the following contrasting ways: The "man of principle" might say: "I have never really become very excited about [say] price controls before, but now, since an action [such as "voting"] has to be taken, I know I ought to act in accordance with my beliefs and feelings on this matter." The other person's "ideal" behavioral choice might result from the following reasoning process: "Sure, I have a viewpoint, but

I cannot be bothered to act upon it; people never do as they ought, anyway." Recently, Schwartz (1968) has found that "Attribution of Responsibility"—that is, the tendency to see oneself responsible for the state of others—correlates moderately with the tendency to behave in accordance with one's beliefs.

We need, then, a personality coefficient for the first term on the right-hand side of our equation. This coefficient represents the degree to which individual i *customarily* acts in accordance with his values, or how heavily the ideal weights in his behavioral choices. Thus our equation becomes

$$\text{Pot. (Beh.}_{ijk}) = f\ (a_i A_{ijk} + U_{ijk} + H_{ijk}),$$

where the new term a_i refers to individual i's "idealism" or propensity to act in accordance with his ideals (without regard to the specific instance).

Let us see what all this means. First of all, we assume that people may have an "ideal" attitude, derived from more abstract values, and unaffected by "practical" considerations, and that it may enter into play, not only in statements that are unrelated to behavior, but also in statements of behavioral intentions, and in behaviors. However, it may be overridden by the higher utility of another behavior, as represented by our second term, and by behavioral stereotype. A self-assessed *behavioral intention* is represented by the same formula as behavior probability, but may contain different second and third terms: When actually confronted with the situation, a person may perceive more potential gains or costs than he anticipated; or he may be more habit-bound (or fixated), and, perhaps to his own chagrin, may resort to customary responses.

The model allows for the specificity of moral conduct while at the same time allowing us to find out the degree to which a person's actions across situations are determined by his principles.

Since we have three major components in our model, any two of them for a resulting behavior may be lower than those for another behavior that did not occur. Not all of these combinational possibilities are of interest; the most meaningful might be the following:

1. *Habit* overrides *moral dictates*. The first term for another behavior was higher than that for the behavior which actually occurred, but the latter had a strong third term.
2. *Habit* overrides *gain*. For another behavior, gain would have been greater, or cost would have been less, as is often the case in fixated or compulsive behavior.
3. *Gain* overrides *morality*. The first term for another behavior was greater than for the one that occurred, but was outweighed by a large second term.

These three types of conflict correspond to those suggested by Kelman and Baron (1968) and by Baron (1967).

Our next chapter will attempt to utilize this model for deriving prescriptions toward the minimization of aggression and prejudice, the resolution of conflicts, and the establishment of socially responsible and cooperative behavior.

XI

Implications for the Model: Factors in the Development and Maintenance of Socially Responsible Behavior

This chapter examines the usefulness of the model for aggressive and altruistic behavior toward a modification of aggression, and the enhancement of nonviolent methods of conflict resolution and, more generally, of socially responsible attitudes and behaviors. It is emphasized that a consideration of cognitive factors in behavior does not preclude the important contributions of affect and emotion.

*I*T MIGHT BE OF VALUE to examine briefly some of the implications of the model for aggressive and altruistic behavior, presented in the preceding chapter, for the establishment of socially responsible values, attitudes, and behaviors and the reduction of violence and interpersonal or intergroup antagonism. As our first application of the model, the resolution of conflicts appears most appropriate for our purposes. Subsequently we shall examine the implications of the model for the problem of reducing aggressive events. With appropriate misgivings, an attempt will then be made to translate the model into prescriptive statements for the enhancement of altruistic values, and the induction of a greater correspondence between ideal, situation-specific attitudes, and behaviors. However weak these prescriptions may appear, little should be required in the way of additional homilies to convince the reader that unless our skills in resolving conflicts peacefully improve drastically, our species faces a very unhappy, and perhaps terminal, period, and, therefore, a small step toward that end is to be preferred to an inert awaiting of ultimate doom.

CONFLICTS AND THEIR RESOLUTION

It has been argued earlier that many instances of interpersonal or intergroup conflicts are fictitious because a rational analysis of possible outcomes would reveal no irreconcilable conflicts of interest. Others are ephemeral; their duration is briefer than the confrontation that threatens to ensue, and by the time the victor prepares to collect his spoils, they have disappeared, or there is now enough of them so that both parties might have benefited. For instance, little imagination is needed to conceive of situations in which one person may become annoyed at another, even though he would be hard put to give a sound reason for his annoyance. If the opportunity exists, an attack might occur in such a situation, but if it is prevented by circumstances, the annoyance will often be found to have simply dissipated. Instances could also be cited of potential confrontation due solely to the ancient custom of responding manfully to affront, without any real conflict of interest. To illustrate a real, but transitory, conflict, let us imagine two suitors disputing, with great ardor, and possibly with physical violence, the favor of a single object of their affections, while she, totally indifferent to (or perhaps unaware of) the custom of knightly contest for the love of a lady, finds happiness with a third, and possibly quite unheroic, gentleman. If the erstwhile cause of aggression has thus dissipated, it might be argued that society as a whole, and certainly the two potential contenders and their families, have registered a net gain from the nonoccurrence of aggression. (Chivalry forbids the speculation that our two contenders, in spite of wounds sustained, might register a net gain through *not* having conquered the disputed prize.)

A strong case could even be made, in many instances, for a moratorium on arguments aimed at presenting respective positions and confounding the opponent. Such arguments do not result in irreversible injury, but they may exacerbate conflict to a greater degree—a conflict, moreover, which essentially may represent no real, enduring conflict of interests, but merely an alleged slight to the psyche, individual or collective, or perhaps the type of temporary conflict of interest which is resolved by the passage of a short period of time.

The existence of some genuine interpersonal or intergroup conflicts is, however, not denied. To argue that it is inappropriate in all but the rarest instances to attack one's fellowman, and to suggest that any society would benefit from greater interpersonal consideration and sympathy, do not imply that a person may not find himself in opposition to another, for various reasons. Unfortunately, some conflicts are real because they entail at least two claimants to the same object, and are of sufficient permanence that to wait for them to disappear of their own accord would imply the passing of generations or, at best, extreme longevity, with only a hollow victory for the last survivor. Such conflicts must in some way find resolution.

A very useful method in the exploration and resolution of conflicts has been that of simulation. Participants assume *roles* in situations representing conflicts between such groups as, say, a labor union and the management of a firm, or between two (or more) nations. The method has serious drawbacks, such as that of being, after all, a microcosmic and obviously "make-believe" situation. "If outcome x occurs, power A attacks power B with 50 megatons" does not adequatey present a real-life (or, more properly, a "real-death") situation. Since the stakes involved are not equivalent, neither is the emotional involvement. But the method seems to function well in separating real from imagined conflicts, in duplicating the decisions to be made, and in evaluating how people estimate probabilities and contingencies. Clearly, it would be folly to accept all findings emerging from these studies as oracular guidelines for action at all times, but they may provide us with just one more tool for dealing with seemingly insoluble problems that arise when irreconcilable interests are in conflict (see Guetzkow et al., 1963).

As was mentioned earlier, there exist some striking examples of how antagonists can learn to cooperate toward a common goal. The mere experience of taking part in situations involving interdependence may involve significant shifts in a person's basic value structure, such as beliefs involving man's obligation toward his fellowman (Sherif et al., 1961; Breer & Locke, 1965).

REDUCTION OF AGGRESSIVE EVENTS

The control and diminution of aggression can be viewed in several ways:

1. A person can learn to view fewer (if any) stimuli as calling for a classification as "noxious" or "aversive." Presumably, he can learn to become less "hostile," or not to carry a "chip on his shoulder."
2. Even where an aversive classification has occurred, he can learn that the situation does not call for an aggressive response.

Both of these instances are subsumed by the first term of the model: the probability that person i will perceive situation j as calling for aggressive behavior k is decreased.

3. We can alter the social and economic payoffs of a situation so that aggression becomes less rewarding.

4. We can aim at reducing the habit strength of aggressive responses and at enhancing the subjective availability of alternative responses, thereby altering the response hierarchy.[1] Cases 3 and 4 refer, of course, to the second and third terms of the model, respectively.

Consider the instance of the rude bus driver who, through ungrammatical but incisive comment about my tendering of a $5 bill, produces an annoyance of sorts. This situation seldom results in a fight: even assuming that I feel confident of my physical prowess in such a confrontation, what stands in the way of my attack are the following factors:

1. I know that I should be committing an unlawful act by attacking.

2. I know that such an attack would also run contrary to the society's norms and expectations regarding appropriate responses to this type of provocation.

3. My reference groups of professional peers, my friends, and my family would view such an attack with disapproval.

Moreover, the nonviolent alternative in such a situation, after a lapse of time during which my injured manhood has had time to recuperate, will usually seem the right and proper response, even though, in another time and place, such insult might have resulted in murder, or possibly a duel. After considered reflection, I shall probably come to the conclusion that a physical encounter would have been a poor risk, given even just a minimal chance that I might have received a disabling or fatal injury. At a more responsible level, I might even allow that even a boor or an oaf is entitled to due process of the law, and that it would have been quite inappropriate for me to cause him pain or injury, without considering what possible difficulties of his own might have caused him to act as he did.

[1] There is one process whereby severe punishment may militate against behavior modification, even where behavioral alternatives are available: The anticipatory anxiety engendered by the stimulus situation may preclude the evaluation of alternative behavioral strategies. Choosing the act highest in the behavioral hierarchy brings on the punishment, but eliminates the more noxious anxiety. Maier (1949) found that behavioral fixation developed in rats when a discrimination had been rendered impossible, but a choice had been forced upon the animal. Solomon and Wynne (1953) obtained findings that appear to contradict our prediction: Dogs given severe shock quickly lost their emotional behavior when given the opportunity to avoid shock by leaving the shock chamber, even though avoidance behavior continued for very long periods without subsequent reinforcement. But Solomon and Wynne's animals were not in the type of situation in which a previously established behavior was punished, or in which a conflict between a strong, unacceptable response competed with a weak, desirable one.

THE INDUCTION OF ALTRUISTIC VALUES AND BEHAVIORS

Throughout this book, we have emphasized our position that altruistic values and behaviors are subject to similar learning processes as are aggressive values and behaviors. However, it was also noted in Chapter IX that the specific cultural circumstances produce practical differences between these two classes in the sense that aggressive values are rarely taught overtly but often implied in behavior; whereas, ideals of cooperation, altruism, and social responsibility form the staple core of religious and secular teachings, but are often contradicted by behaviors which allow the inference of a parallel set of attitudes, translatable as "It is appropriate to *say* that one should go out of one's way for one's fellowman, independent of (or even in contrast with) what one does." Also, we noted that the sheer opportunity for practicing altruistic acts arises perhaps less frequently than that for its counterpart, aggression. It might be advisable, therefore, to consider the implications of our model in the light of these observations so that our application may have greater validity.

Looking at the three terms of the model and their coefficients, we could reasonably call the variables A, U, and H as being specific to the individual as well as the situation: for instance, A_{ijk} means precisely the intrinsic value individual i attaches to behavior k in situation j; U_{ijk} is that behavior's situation-specific utility; and H_{ijk} represents the habit strength of that behavior. The coefficient a_i on the other hand, is seen as a more general characteristic of the individual i, and therefore carries only one subscript. For a given person, there are thus at least four points of leverage at which behavior modification can be undertaken. With regard to the specific situation and the behavior that is desired (1) we can attempt to enhance the intrinsic valuation of that behavior; (2) we can attempt to enhance the person's "pure" attitude toward it; (2) we can enhance the net utility of the behavior by increasing positive payoffs and decreasing negative ones; or (4) through repeated reinforcements without cognitive manipulations, we can simply increase the behavior's habit strength. The drawback to those methods is not hard to see: they are specific to the situation and the behavior, and it is difficult to point to obvious principles that can serve a process of inferential abstraction or induction.

The personality coefficient presents a more promising opportunity: modifying a person's coefficient a_i implies that a change is being effected in the person's general tendency to "weight" or "act in accordance with" his "pure" or "disinterested" attitudes. It is reasonable to ask how such a desirable end can be sought, since the behavioral correlates that are reinforced are of necessity specific rather than generic. If we reinforce a behavior that is in accordance with a belief and runs counter to considerations of utility and to habit, how is the person to abstract from this outcome that what has been reinforced is not the specific attitude, but the "principled act"?

It is suggested that the techniques that might be usefully employed are several. First of all, direct information or tuition, either by itself or in conjunction with other techniques, can at least facilitate mediation of the significant concept that we wish to impart. The most fruitful approach, however, would seem to be to treat this problem of abstracting relevant features in a situation from irrelevant ones in a manner very similar to the method used by Bruner, Goodnow, and Austin (1960) in their concept abstraction tasks. Their subjects were required to formulate the abstract concept on the basis of which target cards were or were not placed within a certain category. We might place before the person whose attitude-behavior correspondence we wish to enhance, a number of situations that conform to a greater or lesser degree with known attitudes, and apply positive evaluation in direct relation to that correspondence. We should then be able to induce in the observer the inference that the relevant quality is not a class of specific attitudes or behaviors, but rather the degree of *correspondence* between them. Having thus encouraged the "general value" of acting in accordance with one's principles or attitudes, the task of teaching, by the various methods described earlier, the specific attitudes deemed desirable stands a better chance of resulting not in a constellation of attitudes only faintly related to behaviors, but in a strong and predictable adherence of behaviors to attitudes.

We must note here that enhancing "principled behavior" implies no value judgment about a particular set of values or attitudes. The only implication is that an individual learns more than meaningless, often hypocritical, assent to a class of values deemed desirable by the society.[2]

THE ROLE OF EMOTION IN INTERPERSONAL EFFECTANCE

It is probably easy to argue convincingly that anger is an emotion whose behavioral effects are usually destructive, and therefore potential aggression ought to be subjected to the "cognitive control" represented by ethical evaluation. But it is here maintained that even potentially beneficial acts ought to be the result of more than merely a "generous impulse," devoid of such cognitive assessment. It might be objected that such an

[2] It is possible to conceive also of a personality coefficient that modifies specific habits. Thus one person may be less "tied to" a single response than another, more "habit-bound," individual. Also, it is possible to modify the manner in which a person translates objective valences into subjective ones. Thus we can learn to fear "social censure" less: "minding" more or less about positive or negative outcomes constitutes such a change in the translation from objective to subjective valences. At this point, however, I have preferred to reduce the variables of the model to a minimum, in order to simplify preliminary tests of its usefulness.

approach would strip a person of all warmth and impulsiveness, and make him into a calculating, cold-blooded individual, incapable not only of anger, but also of love, compassion, and joy.

Such an interpretation of the model would be quite fallacious. The substance of a rational view of behavior is not that man is, or should be, devoid of affectively laden values and attitudes. In fact, it has been argued all along that a prescription for socialization would require not only the teaching of values and attitudes, of which affect is an integral part, but also a propensity to let them play a decisive role in situation-specific behaviors. The antithesis to a rational mode of cognitive functioning need not be warm, impulsive generosity; it might well be caprice, which may be generous at one time, and horribly cruel the next.

The first term of the model, which could be translated as "What should a person like me ideally do in this situation?" is thus not devoid of an emotional, affective component, but is also subject to cognitive assessment. If this seems to lower the incidence of acts of generosity, consider the well-meaning but impulse-dominated person who wreaks emotional havoc wherever he treads, or the passionate proselytizer whose impulses may be noble but may lead to behaviors with various undesirable outcomes. Indeed, we tend to admire more the individual whose generosity is enriched by a full awareness and evaluation of his responsibility to humanity, than the generous, but capricious, scatterbrain who is largely a creature of impulse.

XII

Overview, Observations, and Some Exhortations

The preceding chapters are reviewed briefly, and the important difference between real and imaginary conflicts is stressed once again. In a hortatory mood, the author questions the benefits of deliberately instigated antagonisms alleged to cement group solidarity and enhance effort. It is argued that not only specific classes of aggression but the acceptance of the very notion of violence as a legitimate means toward certain goals may have harmful effects that outweigh all benefits. As to truly "friendly" contest, we know too little to weigh advantages against possible disadvantages.

W E HAVE TRAVELED a long way, and a brief recapitulation may be in order.

First, we have sought to clarify what we really mean by such a term as "aggression," and have concluded that it is meaningless as an individual act, and that it makes sense only if viewed as goal-directed, interpersonal behavior. Secondly, we have questioned the usefulness of traditional, global concepts, which either view aggression as instinctive or relate it to a single antecedent. Both interpretations were rejected, not so much because we felt that we had proved the null hypothesis—that is, that they do not exist—as because their usefulness in the explanation and prediction of that subset of interpersonal behaviors which we defined as "aggression" was deemed minimal.

Our next step was an examination of the role of emotional states, such as anger, in aggressive behavior. After making clear that when we refer to anger we mean not only an autonomic arousal state, but a symbolically mediated labeling of that state and the stimulus configuration, we concluded that anger is related to aggression in a variety of ways; it may affect the classification of the stimulus, it may reduce response alternatives, and it may intensify a selected response, such as aggression But we concluded that there was little point in assuming a one-to-one relationship between an autonomic state having a cognitive label such as "anger" and the class of interpersonal behaviors we have defined as "aggression."

A case was then argued in favor of viewing aggression as resulting from the learning experiences of the aggressor and occasionally the victim from the cultural norms intentionally transmitted to them, and, to a very important degree, from the immediate situational circumstances which entail, as it were, a more or less advantageous "payoff" for an aggressive act, or its alternative.

Our next step was an examination of the determinants that would lead to the personality syndrome classifiable as "prejudice," and the situations furthering its behavioral correlate, discrimination. Again, we concluded that specific prejudices are socially learned, and that the generic tendency toward prejudiced thinking is either internalized through induction based upon observation of a model, or self-inferred from one's own behaviors.

We then looked briefly at some psychological aspects of international conflict and aggression, with the firm conviction that psychology has an important contribution to make, even though we rejected what we consider an oversimplified explanation of intergroup conflict in psychological terms exclusively.

Somewhat belatedly, we outlined our theory of the development of altruistic and cooperative behaviors. Our basic premise was that these behaviors can be profitably viewed as following the same principles of social learning which we consider the major determinant of interpersonal behavior.

In Chapter X we presented a model that attempted to relate attitudes to behaviors; we argued that such a relationship is a more parsimonious and plausible assumption than that of two separate and unrelated behavioral modes, that of "making a statement as to how one would act" and "how one does in fact act."

The model predicts behavior from a knowledge of a person's values his habitual tendency to act in accordance with them, the subjective utilities of anticipated outcomes, and his habit hierarchy.

Chapter XI, finally, suggested some implications of the model for the modification of personality attributes, conflict resolution, and a decrease in the incidence and intensity of aggressive events with a corresponding increase in socially responsible ones.

These tasks may well prove to be loaded with exasperating ambiguities. In the abstract, the prescriptions are obvious and logical (1) Reduce the number and size of stimulus classes to which people respond with aversive emotion. (This, of course, is not equivalent to the prescription of "avoiding frustrations." What is meant here is the classical conditioning, usually of a higher order, whereby, for an individual, certain human stimuli have become aversively conditioned.) (2) Reduce the tangible rewards for aggression, and enhance the rewards for alternative behaviors. (3) Reduce the likelihood of learning aggressive tendencies through imitation, identification, or subtle cultural norms. (4) Reduce situational elicitors, such as emotional or cognitive group support, or the connotations that inhere in certain locales and situations.

But we must not allow ourselves to be deceived by the bland obviousness of our recommendations. Although many instances of conflict usually leading to aggression result from perceptual distortion, and others are so ephemeral as to make a moratorium pending obsolescence the wisest strategy, there remains a core of real conflicts of interest which can be neither reasoned away nor waited out.

Throughout history there has rarely been a period when conflict and war were not glorified as strengtheners of the human fiber and as fertilizers of human ingenuity. Amazingly, much of this attitude prevails even today, in the face of the much greater presence of the horrors of war, and the immense power of new weapons. Nor is such a nostalgic glorification limited to noncombatants. We shall not leap to the conclusion that we are afflicted, as some claim, by a precipitous decline of morals. Let us keep in mind that while Pax Romana reigned serene and Athens attained undying glory, human life was not highly cherished. The Golden Renaissance was characterized by ruthless conflicts among ruling families and factions, and it was not rare to witness murder in the streets, and to see the murderers walk away unhindered. In England executions not only of desperate criminals, but of children convicted of minor thefts were an accepted form of public entertainment less than 200 years ago. Let us, therefore, not be hasty in asserting that our civilization has sunk below any possibility of redemption, and that we are headed inexorably for our well-deserved obliteration.

On the other hand, we can hardly make a strong case for complacency and moral self-righteousness. Our shortcomings are no less reprehensible because they are not unique in history. In addition, science and technology make much of the suffering that was inevitable until quite recently, entirely superfluous, at least in the Western world.

It appears that even the catastrophe of war can provide a welcome novelty to individuals hemmed in by the routine and boredom of family and job and, especially in the case of younger people, meets their desire for adventure and exploration. Recruiters for the military have recently become aware of these motives, and appeals to manliness and adventure now afford additional impact to Uncle Sam's accusing finger. The belief in the merits of violent conflict has even taken the form of generating antagonisms for the express purpose of enhancing individual stamina or group solidarity. Professional football, in the eyes of some of its practitioners, is a case in point.

Examples of deliberately fostered hatred, suspicion, or prejudice for the benefit of either cynical, or sometimes of devoted though misguided leaders, are abundant. We find such artifactual contests for survival, not only among nations—and within a nation, among ethnic subgroups—but also in business, within peer groups, and even in the family. In times of war or lesser conflict, a given society may expend considerable effort through its mass media to convince its members that the nationals of the other group are legitimate targets for aggression, in the belief that hate of an out-group produces a sense of deep loyalty and belongingness among the members of the in-group.

There is some evidence that groups focusing antagonism upon an outsider can develop bonds of intense intragroup loyalty (Lippitt & White, 1958; Chesler & Schmuck, 1963), but the price for such an outcome is disputable on ethical as well as practical grounds.

First of all, the present price of such conflicts may far exceed its putative benefits. Consider the extreme instance of two clans in a southern mountain state who are decimating each other because of an ancient feud. The present participants may no longer remember the event that precipitated a private war lasting for generations. In some cases, they may admit quite freely that the original cause has become irrelevant. Blood must continue to be shed because family loyalty requires it.

Secondly, a *modus vivendi* with the erstwhile target of hostility may have to be found some day; indeed, yesterday's despised enemy may become tomorrow's cherished ally. The situation becomes still more ambiguous if the target is not a group or nation in some relatively remote area of the globe but a part of the very society whose harmony is at stake.

Whatever the merits of competition engendered by intragroup rivalry within a society, it may be necessary to consider the possibility that they are outweighed by the tensions, hostilities, and sufferings they produce. There are thus at least two questions that arise in this context—one ethical, one practical: (1) Is there any justification for enhancing the well-being of the in-group at considerable expense to those not fortunate enough to belong to it? (2) Times and circumstances frequently change definitions of who is a member of the in-group and who is not, and quite often previously despised and feared groups are welcomed as allies and friends. Is it either reasonable or useful to have expended hate against them, and could not the energy so wasted have been utilized more effectively for the well-being of the original in-group?

Furthermore, it could be argued that the animosity arising from real or imagined conflicts produces an ever growing spiral of hostility, resentment, and separation. Stereotypes become more inflexible and unfavorable within the group, and dissent from voicing hatred of the other group is often ruthlessly suppressed. The damage of such a mental set occurs along several dimensions: (1) It facilitates the occurrence of ever more tragic and costly wars. (2) Even though some wars may be precluded by a detente of terror, the thinking processes of individuals obsessed by stereotyped thinking, hate, and fear cannot fail to suffer even in areas seemingly unrelated to the conflict situation. Undoubtedly, some examples to the contrary could be adduced, especially in areas related to the conduct of war. Occasionally, combatants are enriched by intense experiences of cameraderie and altruism, and some artists and thinkers can draw upon the experiences of war itself in order to reflect its horror and futility, and produce masterpieces. More generally, however, creative thought is hampered, both directly because of the physical circumstances afflicting many potential thinkers and artists, and indirectly because of the stifling and depressive climate that such hate and fear produce.

We cannot simply abolish violence and aggression against only a few "chosen" ones. The notion that great loyalty and even self-sacrifice is owed to members of one's in-group, and that no regard at all is owed to anyone outside that group, is not only not conducive to a diminution of violence but may be quite nonfunctional; for the out-group of today may be the in-group of tomorrow. Also, as Wertham points out (1966, p. 333), selective abstentions from violence become totally pointless where there exists no rule of justice, mercy, and orderly dispute. Nonviolence did not save either the lives or the culture of those who were marched to gas chambers not so many years ago. Thus, it is the idea of violence itself, irrespective of the target, which must become anathema.

In this endeavor, all aspects of violence from toy guns to war must be considered. It has been argued that pleasure in violence, even self-sacrifice, cannot be abolished; they are part of human nature. But how do we know that? How is the act of collective violence that is called war different from, and how is it similar to, individual violence like murder? Wertham makes the point that the society's response after the violence has been committed is very important in our understanding of violence, and possibly its control. For after all, if a murderer is, in many instances, not only acquitted but honored, then we may indirectly be proclaiming the idea that violence is not only acceptable but praiseworthy. Wertham (1966) mentions two pitfalls in the study of murderers: (1) to regard murder as a mystery involving elementary irrational forces, and (2) to assume that all murderers are neurotics. However, in making a classification, no distinction is drawn between individual pathology and social phenomena that are unrelated to it.

But where a totally arbitrary murder occurs, as in the case of recent mass murders by rampaging individuals, and in the case of the threefold tragedy which has deprived us of a President and two popular political leaders, the issue is not at all whether the murderer can be shown—after the fact—to have a "psychopathic" or "sociopathic" personality. In many instances, he can. The tragic aspect is that very rarely can such diagnoses help to predict, and perhaps prevent, these occurrences. It must be understood that even a psychopathic personality does not act in a vacuum. It is, again, the social climate that channels his behaviors in a certain direction. When the social climate is such that the killing of humans is treated lightly, and in some respects even considered a desirable or heroic act, then at least some additional factors are given for his catastrophic behavior.

On the other hand, issue must also be taken with Wertham's assertion that violence is synonymous with disorder, and that nonviolence responds to order and law. Unfortunately, the greatest massacre of all times was characterized precisely by an almost fanatical devotion to superficial aspects of regularity, lawfulness, and order. Violence too can be written into lawbooks, and can become the accepted norm of daily interactions.

It is therefore of paramount importance to train the individual to separate negative emotions from harmful or aggressive behavior. There must be expression of negative emotions; but the person must learn that these emotions can be handled in a variety of ways, some of which may even be constructive, but in any case are incompatible with violence.

More generally, society can no longer afford to depict violence and war as high adventure or joyful self-fulfillment. It may well be the greatest fallacy to reason that a preparation for war is, through deterrence, a sure path to peace. Such a course may have some usefulness as a bridgegap, but its long-range prognosis—both in terms of the psychological habituation to such a continued state of mutual terror and, in a merely probabilistic sense, of the chances for miscalculation or accident—is not encouraging.

Nothing said in this or the preceding chapters should be construed as discouragement or disapproval of any type of "friendly" contest or comparison, even though there are studies indicating that competition in school, contrary to popular belief, is not necessarily beneficial for performance. It must be admitted that we know far too little at this point to assert categorically that competition or contest never has desirable consequences in terms of enhancing useful motivation and performance. But even while this question is open, great care should be taken with respect to the situation in which such competition is encouraged and to the means by which this is done. Even athletic events sometimes induce in the contestants a deep hatred of the opponent and a will to destroy him—an attitude that is sometimes deliberately fostered, for example, by successful football coaches. Although no real efforts at exterminating others on the football field may result, such techniques may strengthen existing attitudes as to what is appropriate behavior toward an opponent—athletic, business, political, or otherwise.

Perhaps even language use in our beneficial endeavors could undergo some changes. True, "killing poor people" is an unusual interpretation of the War on Poverty, used only by (several) comedians. But is it really true that we cannot find a phrase or a word in our language that describes an intense, concerned, and dedicated effort toward eradicating an evil, without having to resort to the language of warfare?

It is most important to disclaim at this point any intention to minimize the role of affect or emotion in the conduct of life. The answer, clearly, is not to make individuals incapable of emotion, in an attempt to bring rationality to the fore. The emotionless individual, even though highly intelligent, is deficient in the fulfillment he can attain, or can give to others. More important, it appears that organisms deliberately deprived of emotional development also suffer intellectual and, perhaps, physical impairment. An emotionally "potent" individual, therefore, clearly must have a *capacity* for anger. Indeed, it is difficult to imagine even the most righteous and peace-loving individual without the ability to feel appropriate indignation, say, in the face of rank injustice.

What must be learned is that there are behaviors other than aggression appropriate to emotion, as well as in quite genuine conflicts, that aggression is socially reprehensible, and for that and other reasons, unacceptable.

How, then, can we summarize the conclusions offered in this book and what consequences can we draw?

1. It would seem, first of all, that the large bulk of man's antagonism to man is the outcome of situational pressures, even though man's personality plays a noticeable part, especially with regard to readiness with which he accepts aggressive solutions in conflict situations.

2. Without wishing to minimize man's stature, we must realize at least that it is not at all difficult to induce, in intelligent, cultured individuals, a readiness to inflict pain, torture, and even death, under a minimal pretext. This realization need not result in despair, or in a rejection of man as a suitable inhabitant for this planet. Instead, we must view this propensity as one of the innumerable aspects that are peculiar to the species of man.

3. There is a brighter obverse to this painful realization; namely that man can be moved toward good as readily as toward evil. Even small children can learn to behave with consideration, altruism, and even self-sacrifice, toward other individuals. It is up to us to make sure teachings more prevalent than they now are, and to reduce the attractiveness and applicability of violent and discriminatory behavior that our society now purveys in so many respects.

4. There are no simple solutions. Some conflicts are imaginary; others are real in that goal attainment by one party at least partially precludes goal attainment by the other. Essentially, however, aggression, especially now, when the price of such aggression has transcended all imaginable bounds of utility, cannot ever be considered as an acceptable solution for a conflict, however real its existence. If we are to survive, not only in the physical sense of the word, but as a civilization, we must find alternative ways of dealing with such conflicts.

5. There is little sense in limiting our exploration of such conflict resolutions to the peripheries of our lives. We cannot hope to have more than a detente of terror with other nations if we cannot find in our family, in our peer groups, and in our political spheres ways of settling disputed issues other than by attacking, and in some way or other seeking to destroy each other.

6. It is unrealistic, cowardly, and in all probability, incorrect to assign our present desperate dilemmas to "human nature." We do not know what human nature is, and therefore cannot plead this alibi for a failure to examine the problems with which we must in the course of our lives come to grips.

7. This does not mean that there is no place for emotion in our behavior. On the contrary, it is emotion that must help us to feel a sense of revulsion when we witness the suffering of a fellowman or, more important still, when we are called upon to inflict it.

8. It is often said that the social scientist, or the scientist in general, cannot determine what man's ultimate values should be. All that the scientist can do is give some guidance in how such values might be attained. There is a serious flaw in this argument. No values at all can be attained by man after he has destroyed himself. It is only through the preservation of man, and by placing him in a position where a greater number of alternatives is available to him, that a choice of values is possible. It may well be that the social scientist may provide some help in ensuring that such a choice, whoever will be called upon to make it, will at some time in the future be possible.

REFERENCES

Adams, B. N. Interaction theory and the social network. *Sociometry,* 1967, **30,** 64–78.

Adelson, J. A study of minority group authoritarianism. *Journal of Abnormal and Social Psychology* 1953, 48, 477–485.

Adorno, T. W., Frenkel-Brunswik, E., Levinson, D. J., & Sanford, R. N. *The authoritarian personality.* New York: Harper & Bros., 1950.

Allport, G. *The nature of prejudice.* Reading, Mass.: Addison-Wesley, 1954.

Andreski, S. Origins of war. In J. D. Carthy and F. J. Ebling (Eds.), *The natural history of aggression.* New York: Academic Press, 1964.

Arendt, H. *Eichmann in Jerusalem: A report on the banality of evil.* New York: Viking Press, 1963.

Aronfreed, J. The concept of internalization. In D. A. Goslin and D. C. Glass (Eds.), *Handbook on socialization theory.* Chicago: Rand-McNally, 1967.

Aronfreed, J., & Paskal, V. Altruism, empathy and the conditioning of positive affect. Unpublished manuscript, University of Pennsylvania, 1965.

Azrin, N. H. Unpublished study, 1964.

Azrin, N. H., & Hutchinson, R. R. Unpublished study, 1963.

Azrin, N. H., Hutchinson, R. R., & Sallery, R. D. Pain-aggression toward inanimate objects. *Journal of Experimental Analysis of Behavior,* 1964, **7,** 233–237.

Bandura, A. Vicarious processes: A case of no-trial learning. In L. Berkowitz (Ed.), *Advances in experimental social psychology.* Vol. 2. New York: Academic Press, 1965.

Bandura, A., & Huston, A. C. Identification as a process of incidental learning. *Journal of Abnormal and Social Psychology,* 1961, **63,** 311–318.

Bandura, A., Ross, D., & Ross, S. A. Transmission of aggression through imitation of aggressive models. *Journal of Abnormal and Social Psychology,* 1961, **63,** 575–582.

Bandura, A., Ross, D., & Ross S. A. Imitation of film-mediated aggressive models. *Journal of Abnormal and Social Psychology,* 1963, **66,** 3–11. (a)

Bandura, A., Ross, D., & Ross, S. A. Vicarious reinforcement and imitation. *Journal of Abnormal and Social Psychology,* 1963, **67,** 601–607. (b)

Bandura, A., & Walters, R. H. *Social learning and personality development.* New York: Holt, Rinehart and Winston, 1963.

Bard, P., & Mountcastle, V. B. Some forebrain mechanism involved in expression of rate with special reference to suppression of angry behavior. *Proceedings of Association for Research in Nervous and Mental Disease,* 1947, **27,** 362–404.

Bard, P., & Rioch, D. McK. A study of four cats deprived of neocortex and additional portions of the forebrain. *Johns Hopkins Hospital Bulletin,* 1937, **60,** 73–147.

Baron, R. M. A functional analysis of attitude-discrepant behavior. *Proceedings of the Annual Convention of the American Psychological Association,* 1967.

Barzun, J. *Race, a study in superstition.* New York: Harper & Row, 1965.

Bayton, J. A. The racial stereotypes of Negro college students. *Journal of Abnormal and Social Psychology,* 1941, **36**, 390–402.

Beach, F. A. Bisexual mating behavior in the male rat: Effects of castration and hormone administration. *Physiological Zoology,* 1945, **18**, 390–402.

Beeman, E. A. The effects of male hormone on aggressive behavior in mice. *Physiological Zoology,* 1947, **20**, 373–405.

Bem, D. J. Self-perception: An alternative interpretation of cognitive dissonance phenomena. *Psychological Review,* 1967, **74**, 183–200.

Benedict, R. *Race: Science and politics.* New York: Viking Press, 1943.

Benedict, R. *Patterns of culture.* New York: Mentor Books, 1946.

Berkowitz, L. Manifest hostility level and hostile behavior. *Journal of Social Psychology,* 1960, **52**, 165–171.

Berkowitz, L. *Aggression: A social psychological anlaysis.* New York: McGraw-Hill, 1962.

Berkowitz, L. Aggressive cues in aggressive behavior and hostility catharsis. *Psychological Review,* 1964, **71**, 104–122.

Berkowitz, L. Response to Stone. *Journal of Personality and Social Psychology,* 1965, **2**, 757–758. (a)

Berkowitz, L. Some aspects of observed aggression. *Journal of Personality and Social Psychology,* 1965, **2**, 359–369. (b)

Berkowitz, L., & Connor, W. H. Success, failure and social responsibility. *Journal of Personality and Social Psychology,* 1966, **4**, 664–669.

Berkowitz, L., & Daniels, L. R. Responsibility and dependency. *Journal of Abnormal and Social Psychology,* 1963, **66**, 429–436.

Berkowitz, L., & Daniels, L. R. Affecting the salience of the social responsibility norm: Effects of past help on the response to dependency relationships. *Journal of Abnormal and Social Psychology,* 1964, **68**, 275–281.

Berkowitz, L., & Friedman, P. Some social class differences in helping behavior. *Journal of Abnormal and Social Psychology.* 1967, **5**, 217–225.

Berkowitz, L., & Geen, R. G. Film violence and the cue properties of available targets. *Journal of Personality and Social Psychology,* 1966, **3**, 525–530.

Berkowitz, L., Geen, R. G. Stimulus qualities of the target of aggression: A further study. *Journal of Personality and Social Psychology,* 1967, **5**, 363–364.

Berkowitz, L., & Green, J. A. The stimulus qualities of the scapegoat. *Journal of Abnormal and Social Psychology,* 1962, **64**, 293–300.

Berkowitz, L., & Holmes, D. C. The generalization of hostility to disliked objects. *Journal of Personality,* 1959, **27**, 565–577.

Berkowitz, L., & Holmes, D. S. A further investigation of hostility generalization to disliked objects. *Journal of Personality,* 1960, **28**, 427–442.

Berkowitz, L., Klanderman, S. B., & Harris, R. Effects of experimenter awareness and sex of subject and experimenter on reactions to dependency relationships. *Sociometry,* 1964, **27**, 327–337.

Berkowitz, L., & LePage, A. Weapons as aggression-eliciting stimuli. *Journal of Personality and Social Psychology,* 1967, **7,** 202–207.

Berkowitz, L., & Lutterman, K. G. The traditional socially responsible personality. *Public Opinion Quarterly,* 1968, **32,** 169–185.

Berlyne, D. E. *Conflict, arousal and curiosity.* New York: McGraw-Hill, 1960.

Bernard, J. The sociological study of conflict. In *The nature of conflict.* Paris: UNESCO, 1957.

Bettelheim, B., & Janowitz, M. *Dynamics of prejudice.* New York: Harper & Bros., 1950.

Bixenstine, V. E., Potash, H. M., & Wilson, K. V. Effects of level of cooperative choice by the other player on choices in a prisoner's dilemma game (Pt. 1). *Journal of Abnormal and Social Psychology,* 1963, **66,** 308–313.

Brady, J. V. Emotional behavior. In J. Field, H. W. Magoun, and E. V. Hall (Eds.), *Handbook of physiology.* Vol. 3. Washington: American Physiological Society, 1960.

Breer, P. E., & Locke, E. A. *Task experience as a source of attitudes.* Homewood, Ill: Dorsey, 1965.

Brehm, J. *A theory of psychological reactance.* New York: Academic Press, 1966.

Brehm, M. W., Back, K. W., & Bogdonoff, M. D. A physiological effect of cognitive dissonance under stress and deprivation. *Journal of Abnormal and Social Psychology,* 1964, **69,** 303–310.

Brogden, H. E. A factor analysis of 40 character traits. *Psychological Monographs,* 1940, **52**(Whole No. 234).

Bronfenbrenner, U. The mirror image in Soviet-American relations. *Journal of Social Issues,* 1961, **17,** 45–46.

Brown, J. S., & Farber, I. E. Emotions conceptualized as intervening variables with suggestions toward a theory of frustration. *Psychological Bulletin,* 1951, **48,** 465–495.

Brown, R. *Social psychology.* New York: Free Press, 1965.

Bruner, J. S., Goodnow, J. J., & Austin, G. A. *A study of thinking.* New York: Wiley, 1960.

Buss, A. *The psychology of aggression.* New York: Wiley, 1961.

Cannon, W. B. *Bodily changes in pain, hunger, fear, and rage.* New York: Appleton, 1929.

Cannon, W. B., & Britton, S. W. Studies on the conditions of activity in endocrine glands. XX. The influence of motivation and emotion on medulliadrenal secretion. *American Journal of Physiology,* 1927, **79,** 433–464.

Cassirer, E. *An essay on man.* New Haven: Yale University Press, 1944.

Cassirer, E. *The myth of the state.* New Haven: Yale University Press, 1946.

Chesler, M., & Schmuck, R. Participant observation in super-patriot discussion groups. *Journal of Social Issues,* 1963, **19,** 18–30.

Chomsky, N. A review of B. F. Skinner's verbal behavior. *Language,* 1959, **1,** 26–58.

Christie, R., & Jahoda, M. (Eds.) Studies in the scope and method of *The Authoritarian Personality.* Glencoe, Ill.: Free Press, 1954.

Clark, K. B., & Clark, M. P. Racial identification and preference in Negro children. In T. M. Newcomb and E. L. Hartley (Eds.), *Readings in social psychology*. New York: Holt, Rinehart and Winston, 1947.

Cohen, A. R. Communication discrepancy and attitude change: A dissonance theory approach. *Journal of Personality*, 1959, **27**, 286–389.

Covain, M. R. Role of emotional stress in the survival of adrenalectomized rats given replacement therapy. *Journal of Clinical Endocrinology*, 1949, **9**, 678.

Crowne, D., & Marlowe, D. *The approval motive*. New York: Wiley, 1964.

Daniels, L. R., & Berkowitz, L. Liking and response to dependency relationships. *Human Relations*, 1963, **16**, 141–148.

Darley, J., & Latané, B. Diffusion of responsibility in emergency situations. *Proceedings of the Annual Convention of the American Psychological Association*, 1966.

Darlington, R. B., & Macker, C. E. Displacement of guilt-produced altruistic behavior. *Journal of Personality and Social Psychology*, 1966, **4**, 442–443.

Darwin, C. *The expression of emotions in man and animals*. Chicago: University of Chicago Press, 1965.

De Charms, R., & Wilkins, E. J. Some effects of verbal expression of hostility. *Journal of Abnormal and Social Psychology*, 1963, **66**, 462–470.

Deutsch, M. Trust, trustworthiness, and the F scale. *Journal of Abnormal and Social Psychology*, 1960, **61**, 138–140.

Deutsch, M. Cooperation and trust: Some theoretical notes. In M. R. Jones (Ed.), *Nebraska symposium on motivation*. Lincoln: University of Nebraska Press, 1962.

Deutsch, M., & Krauss, R. M. The effect of threat upon interpersonal bargaining. *Journal of Abnormal and Social Psychology*, 1960, **61**, 181–189.

Deutsch, M., & Krauss, R. M. Studies of interpersonal bargaining. *Conflict Resolution*, 1962, **6**, 52–76.

Dollard, J., Miller, N., Doob, L., Mowrer, O. H., & Sears, R. R. *Frustration and aggression*. New Haven: Yale University Press, 1939.

Edwards, A. L. *The social desirability variable in personality assessment and research*. New York: Dryden Press, 1957.

Edwards, W. A theory of decision making. *Psychological Bulletin*, 1954, **51**, 385–417.

Feierabend, R. L., & Feierabend, I. K. Aggressive behaviors within politics: A cross-national study. Paper presented at the meeting of the American Psychological Association, Chicago, September 1965.

Feshbach, S. The drive-reducing function of fantasy behavior. *Journal of Abnormal and Social Psychology*, 1955, **59**, 3–11.

Feshbach, S. The catharsis hypothesis and some consequences of interaction with aggressive and neutral play objects. *Journal of Personality*, 1956, **24**, 449–462.

Feshbach, S. Aggression. Unpublished manuscript, University of California, 1967.

Festinger, L. A theory of social comparison processes. *Human Relations,* 1954, **7,** 117–140.

Festinger, L. *A theory of cognitive dissonance.* Evanston, Ill.: Row, Peterson, 1957.

Festinger, L. *Conflict, decision and dissonance.* Stanford: Stanford University Press, 1964.

Festinger, L., Schachter, S., & Back, K. *Social pressures in informal groups: A study of human factors in housing.* New York: Harper & Bros., 1950.

Fischer, A. Sharing in preschool children as a function of amount and type of reinforcement. *Genetic psychology monographs,* 1963, **68,** 215–245.

Frazer, J. G. *The golden bough: A study in magic and religion.* (3rd ed.) New York: Macmillan, 1935.

Freud, A. *The ego and the mechanisms of defense.* New York: International University Press, 1946.

Freud, S. On narcissism: An introduction. 1914. In S. Freud, *Collected papers.* Vol. 4, pp. 30–50. London: Hogarth Press, 1925.

Freud, S. *Beyond the pleasure principle.* Translated by James Strachey. New York: Liveright, 1950. (First published in 1920 in German: *Jenseits des Lustprinzips.*)

Gilbert, G. M. Stereotype persistence and change among college students. *Journal of Abnormal and Social Psychology,* 1951, **46,** 245–254.

Glickman, S. E., & Schiff, B. B. A biological theory of reinforcement. *Psychological Review,* 1967, **74,** 81–109.

Goranson, R. E., & Berkowitz, L. Reciprocity and social responsibility reactions to prior help. *Journal of Personality and Social Psychology,* 1966, **3,** 227–232.

Gouldner, A. W. The norm of reciprocity: A preliminary statement. *American Sociological Review,* 1960, **25,** 161–178.

Greenglass, E. R. The effects of prior help and hindrance on willingness to help another: Reciprocity or social responsibility. Unpublished doctoral dissertation, University of Toronto, 1967.

Greenspoon, J. The reinforcing effect of two spoken sounds on the frequency of two responses. *American Journal of Psychology,* 1955, **50,** 409–416.

Guetzkow, H., Alger, C. F., Brody, R. A., Noel, R. C., & Snyder, R. C. *Simulation in international relations: Developments for research and training.* Englewood Cliffs, N.J.: Prentice–Hall, 1963.

Guthrie, E. R. Association and the law of effect. *Psychological Review,* 1940. **47,** 127–148.

Haldane, J. B. S. *The causes of evolution.* New York: Longmans, 1935.

Harris, D. B. A scale for measuring attitudes of social responsibility in children. *Journal of Abnormal and Social Psychology,* 1957, **55,** 322–326.

Hartshorne, H., & May, M. A. *Studies in the nature of character.* Vol 1. *Studies in deceit.* New York: Macmillan, 1928.

Hebb, D. O. *A textbook of psychology.* Philadelphia: Saunders, 1966.

Heider, F., *The psychology of international relations.* New York: Wiley, 1946.

Hilgard, E. R., & Bower, G. H. *Theories of learning.* (3rd ed.) New York: Appleton-Century-Crofts, 1966.

Hinde, R. A. Some recent studies in ethology. In S. Koch (Ed.), *Psychology: A study of a science.* Vol. 2, pp. 561–610. New York: McGraw-Hill, 1959.

Hoffer, E. *The true believer.* New York: Mentor books, 1958. (First published 1951 by Harper & Brothers.)

Hokanson, J. E., & Shetler, S. The effect of overt aggression on physiological arousal level. *Journal of Abnormal and Social Psychology,* 1961, **63,** 446–448.

Homans, G. C. *Social behavior: Its elementary forms.* New York: Harcourt, Brace & World, 1961.

Horowitz, E. L. The development of attitudes toward the Negro. *Archives of Psychology,* 1936, **194** (entire issue).

Hovland, C., & Sears, R. Minor studies in aggression: VI. Correlation of lynchings with economic indices. *Journal of Psychology,* 1940, **9,** 301–310.

Hull, C. L. *Principles of behavior.* New York: Appleton-Century-Crofts, 1943.

Hunt, J. McV., Cole, H. W., & Reis, E. E. Situational cues distinguishing anger, fear and sorrow. *American Journal of Psychology,* 1958, **71,** 136–151.

Janis, I. L. Personality correlates of susceptibility to persuasion. *Journal of Personality,* 1954, **22,** 504–518.

Janis, I. L., & Field, P. B. A behavioral assessment of persuasibility: Consistency of individual differences. In C. I. Hovland and I. L. Janis (Eds.), *Personality and persuasibility.* New Haven: Yale University Press, 1959. Pp. 29–54.

Johnson, C. S. *Growing up in the black belt.* Washington, D.C. American Council on Education, 1941.

Jones, E. E., & Davis, K. E. From acts to dispositions. In L. Berkowitz (Ed.), *Advances in experimental social psychology.* Vol. 2. New York: Academic Press, 1965.

Kagan, J. Socialization of aggression and the perception of parents in fantasy. *Child Development,* 1958, **29,** 311–320.

Katz, D. & Braly, K. W. Racial stereotypes of 100 college students. *Journal of Abnormal and Social Psychology,* 1933, **28,** 280–290.

Kaufmann, H. Definitions and methodology in the study of aggression. *Psychological Bulletin,* 1965, **64,** 351–364.

Kaufmann, H. Social psychological analysis of hate propaganda. In *Report to the Minister of Justice of the Special Committee on Hate Propaganda in Canada.* Ottawa: Queen's Printer, 1966.

Kaufmann, H. *Introduction to the study of human behavior.* Philadelphia: Saunders, 1968.

Kaufmann, H. The unconcerned bystander. In *Proceedings of the Annual Convention of the American Psychological Association,* 1968.

Kaufmann, H. A model for attitude-behavior discrepancies. Unpublished manuscript, Hunter College, 1969.

Kaufmann, H., & Feshbach, S. Displaced aggression and its modification through exposure to anti-aggressive communications. *Journal of Abnormal and Social Psychology,* 1963, **67,** 79–83. (a)

Kaufmann, H., & Feshbach, S. The influence of anti-aggressive communications upon the response to provocation. *Journal of Personality,* 1963, **31,** 428–444. (b)

Kaufmann, H., & Marcus, A. Aggression as a function of similarity between aggressor and victim. *Perceptual and Motor Skills,* 1965, **20,** 1013–1020.

Kelley, H. H., & Volkart, E. H. The resistance to change of group-anchored attitudes. *American Sociological Review,* 1952, **17,** 453–465.

Kelman, H. C., & Baron, R. M. Determinants of resolving inconsistency dilemmas: A functional analysis. In R. P. Abelson, E. Aronson, W. J. McGuire, T. M. Newcomb, and P. H. Tannenbaum (Eds.), *Inconsistency theories.* Chicago: Rand-McNally, 1968.

Kelman, H. C., & Hovland, C. I. "Reinstatement" of the communicator in delayed measurement of opinion change. *Journal of Abnormal and Social Psychology,* 1953, **48,** 327–335.

Keniston, K. *The uncommitted.* New York: Harcourt, Brace & World, 1965.

Kenny, D. T. *An experimental test of the catharsis hypothesis of aggression.* Ann Arbor, Mich.: University Microfilms, 1953.

Kline, C. L. Killing for Christmas. *The Progressive,* 1966, **30,** 24–27.

Klineberg, O. Tensions affecting international understanding. *Social Science Research Council Bulletin,* 1950, No. 62.

Klineberg, O. *The human dimension in international relations.* New York: Holt, Rinehart and Winston, 1965.

Kohlberg, L. The development of children's orientations toward a moral order: I. Sequence in the development of moral thought, *Vita Humana,* 1963, **6,** 11–33.

Kohlberg, L. Development of moral character and moral ideology. In M. L. Hoffman and I. W. Hoffman (Eds.), *Review of child development research.* Vol. 1. New York: Russell Sage Foundation, 1964.

Krech, D., Crutchfield, R. S., & Ballachey, E. L. *The individual in society.* New York: McGraw-Hill, 1959.

Kropotkin, P. *Mutual aid.* New York: Doubleday, 1902.

Langer, S. K. *Philosophy in a new key.* Cambridge: Harvard University Press, 1948.

Lasswell, H. D. *Psychopathology and politics.* Chicago: University of Chicago Press, 1930.

Lasswell, H. D. *Power and personality.* New York: Norton, 1948.

Latané, B., & Darley, J. Group inhibition of bystander intervention in emergencies. *Proceedings of the Annual Convention of the American Psychological Association,* 1966.

Lesser, G. S. Extrapunitiveness and ethnic attitude. *Journal of Abnormal and Social Psychology,* 1958, **56,** 281.

Levison, P. K., & Flynn, J. P. The objects attacked by cats during stimulation of the hypothalamus. *Animal Behavior,* 1965, **13,** 217–220.

Lewin, K. *Resolving social conflicts.* New York: Harper & Bros., 1948.

Lewin, K., Lippitt, R., & White, R. K. Patterns of aggressive behavior in experimentally created "social climates." *Journal of Social Psychology,* 1939, **10,** 271–299.

Lewis, M., & Richman, S. Social encounters and their affect on subsequent social reinforcement. *Journal of Abnormal and Social Psychology,* 1964, **69,** 253–257.

Linton, H., & Graham, E. Personality correlates of persuasibility. In C. I. Hovland and I. L. Janis (Eds.), *Personality and persuasibility.* New Haven: Yale University Press, 1959.

Lippitt, R. & White, R. K. An experimental study of leadership and group life. In E. E. Maccoby, T. M. Newcomb, and E. L. Hartley (Eds.), *Readings in social psychology.* (3rd ed.) New York: Holt, Rinehart & Winston, 1958.

Lorenz, K. Ueber die Bildung des Instinktbegriffes. *Naturwissenschaften,* 1937, **25,** 289–300; 307–318; 324–331.

Lorenz, K. *On aggression.* New York: Harcourt, Brace & World, 1966. (Original publication: *Des sogenannte Böse.* Vienna, Austria; Dr. G. Borothaschoeler, 1963.

MacCorquodale, K., & Meehl, P. E. On a distinction between hypothetical constructs and intervening variables, *Psychological Review,* 1948, **55,** 95–107.

Magaziner, D. E. The effects of insecurity upon aggressive responsiveness, *Dissertation Abstracts,* 1961, **22,** 1955.

Maier, N. R. F. *Frustration: The study of behavior without a goal.* Ann Arbor, Mich.: University of Michigan Press, 1949.

Malinowski, B. *The foundation of faith and morals.* London: Oxford University Press, 1936.

Mandler, G. Emotion. In R. Brown, E. Galanter, E. H. Hess, and G. Mandler (Eds.), *New directions in psychology.* New York: Holt, Rinehart and Winston, 1962.

Maslow, A. H. Deprivation, threat, and frustration. *Psychological Review,* 1941, **48,** 364–366.

McDougall, W. *An introduction to social psychology.* London: Methuen, 1908.

Mead, G. H. *Mind, self, and society.* Chicago: University of Chicago Press, 1934.

Merton, R. K. Discrimination and the American creed. In R. W. MacIver (Ed.), *Discrimination and national welfare.* New York: Harper & Bros., 1949.

Midlarsky, E., & Bryan, J. H. Training charity in children. *Journal of Personality and Social Psychology,* 1967, **5,** 408–415.

Milgram, S. Behavioral study of obedience. *Journal of Abnormal and Social Psychology,* 1963, **67,** 371–378.

Milgram, S. Group pressure and action against a person. *Journal of Abnormal and Social Psychology,* 1964, **69,** 137–143.

Milgram, S. Liberating effects of group pressure. *Journal of Personality and Social Psychology,* 1965, **1,** 127–134.

Miller, G. A., Galanter, E. H., & Pribram, K. *Plans and the structure of behavior.* New York: Holt, 1960.

Miller, N. E., The Frustration-aggression hypothesis. *Psychological Review,* 1941, **48,** 337–342.

Miller, N. E. Studies of fear as an acquirable drive. I. Fear as motivation and fear reduction as reinforcement in the learning of new responses. *Journal of Experimental Psychology*, 1948, **38**, 89–101.

Miller, N. E. Liberalization of basic S–R concepts: Extensions to conflict behavior, motivation, and social learning. In S. Koch (Ed.), *Psychology: A study of a science*. Vol. 2, pp. 196–202. New York: McGraw-Hill, 1959.

Miller, N. E., & Dollard, J. C. *Social learning and imitation*. New Haven: Yale University Press, 1941.

Montagu, A. *On being human*. New York: Hawthorn Books, 1950.

Montagu, A. *Race, science, and humanity*. Princeton, N.J.: Van Nostrand, 1963.

Mowrer, O. H. *Learning theory and personality dynamics*. New York: Ronald Press, 1950.

Mowrer, O. H. *Learning theory and the symbolic processes*. New York: Wiley, 1960. (a).

Mowrer, O. H. *Learning theory and behavior*. New York: Wiley, 1960. (b).

Mowrer, O. H. Civilization and its malcontents. *Psychology Today,* 1967, **1**, 48–52.

Munn, N. L. The effect of the knowledge of the situation upon judgement of emotion from facial expressions. *Journal of Abnormal and Social Psychology*, 1940, **35**, 324–338.

Murstein, B. I. The effect of amount of possession of the trait of hostility on accuracy of perception of hostility in others. *Journal of abnormal and Social Psychology*, 1961, **62**, 216–220.

Myrdal, G. *An American dilemma*. New York: Harper & Bros., 1944.

Newcomb, T. M. Autistic hostility and social reality. *Human Relations,* 1947, **1**, 69–86.

Newcomb, T. M. Attitude development as a function of reference groups. In E. E. Maccoby, T. M. Newcomb, and E. L. Hartley. (Eds.), *Readings in social psychology*. New York: Holt, 1958.

O'Kelly, L. E., & Steckle, L. C. A note on long-enduring emotional responses in the rat. *Journal of Psychology*, 1939, **8**, 125–131.

Osgood, C. E., Suci, G. J., & Tannenbaum, P. H. *The measurement of meaning*. Urban, Ill.: University of Illinois Press, 1957.

Oxford Universal Dictionary. (3rd ed.) New York: Clarendon Press, 1955.

Pastore, N. The role of arbitrariness in the frustration-aggression hypothesis. *Journal of Abnormal and Social Psychology*, 1952, **47**, 728–731.

Peak, H. Psychological structure and psychological activity. *Psychological Review*, 1958, **65**, 325–347.

Peak, H. The effects of aroused motivations or attitudes. *Journal of Abnormal and Social Psychology*, 1960, **61**, 463–464.

Pepitone, A. Attributions of causality, social attitudes, and cognitive matching processes. In R. Tagiuri, and L. Petrullo (Eds.), *Person perception and interpersonal behavior*. Stanford, Calif.: Stanford University Press, 1958.

Pepitone, A. *Attraction and hostility*. New York: Atherton Press, 1964.

Pepitone, A., & Reichling, G. Group cohesiveness and the expression of hostility. *Human Relations*, 1955, **8**, 327–337.

Peters, R. S. *The concept of motivation.* (2nd ed.) New York: Humanities Press, 1960.

Pettigrew, T. F. Regional differences in anti-Negro prejudice. *Journal of Abnormal and Social Psychology*, 1959, **59**, 28–35.

Pettigrew, T. F. *A profile of the Negro American.* Princeton, N.J.: Van Nostrand, 1964.

Piaget, J. *The moral judgement of the child.* London: Kegan Paul, 1932.

Rapoport, A., & Chammah, A. M. *Prisoner's dilemma: A study in conflict and cooperation.* Ann Arbor, Mich.: University of Michigan Press, 1965.

Razran, G. Ethnic dislikes and stereotypes: A laboratory study. *Journal of Abnormal and Social Psychology*, 1950, **45**, 7–27.

Redl, F. The phenomenon of contagion and "shock effect" in group psychotherapy. In K. R. Eissler (Ed.), *Searchlights on delinquency.* New York: International University Press, 1949.

Redl, F., & Wineman, D. *Children Who Hate.* New York: Collier Books, 1962.

Reiss, P. J. The extended kinship system: Correlates of and attitudes on frequency of interaction. *Marriage and Family Living*, 1962, **24**, 334.

Rheingold, H. L., Gewirtz, J. C., & Ross, H. W. Social conditioning of vocalization in infants. *Journal of Comparative Physiological psychology*, 1959, **52**, 68–73.

Riesman, D., Glazer, N., & Denney, R. *The lonely crowd.* New Haven: Yale University Press, 1950.

Rosenbaum, M. E. The effect of stimulus and background factors on the volunteering response. *Journal of Abnormal and Social Psychology*, 1956, **53**, 118–121.

Rosenbaum, M. E., & deCharms, R. Direct and vicarious reduction of hostility. *Journal of Abnormal and Social Psychology*, 1960, **60**, 105–111.

Rosenberg, M. Cognitive structure and attitudinal effect. *Journal of Abnormal and Social Psychology*, 1956, **53**, 367–372.

Rosenberg, M., & Hovland, C. I. Cognitive, affective and behavioral components of attitudes. In M. Rosenberg, C. I. Hovland, W. J. McGuire, R. P. Abelson, and J. W. Brehm, *Attitude organization and change.* New Haven: Yale University Press, 1960.

Rosenhan, D., & White, G. M. Observation and rehearsal as determinants of prosocial behavior. *Journal of Personality and Social Psychology*, 1967, **5**, 424–431.

Rosenzweig, S. An outline of frustration theory. In J. McV. Hunt (Ed.), *Personality and the behavior disorders.* New York: Ronald Press, 1944.

Sarbin, T. R. Ontology recapitulates philology: The mythic nature of anxiety. *American Psychologist*, 1968, **23**, 411–418.

Sarbin, T. R., & Allen, V. Role theory. In *The handbook of social psychology.* (2nd ed.) (Vol. I) Reading, Mass.: Addison-Wesley, 1968.

Sartre, J.-P. *Anti-Semite and Jew.* New York: Schocken, 1948.

Schachter, S., & Singer, J. E. Cognitive, social and physiological determinants of emotional state. *Psychological Review,* 1962, **69,** 379–399.

Schachter, S., & Wheeler, L. Epinephrine, chlorpromazine, and amusement. *Journal of Abnormal and Social Psychology,* 1962, **65,** 121–128.

Schoenfeld, W. M. An experimental study of some problems relating to stereotypes. *Archives of Psychology,* 1942, No. 270.

Schreiner, L., & Kling, A. Rhinencaphalon and behavior. *American Journal of Physiology,* 1956, **184,** 486–490.

Schwartz, S. H. Words, deeds, and the perception of consequences and responsibility in action situations. *Journal of Personality and Social Psychology,* 1968, **10,** 232–242.

Scott, J. P. *Aggression.* Chicago: University of Chicago Press, 1958.

Scott, J. P., & Fredericson, E. The causes of fighting in mice and rats. *Physiological Zoology.* 1951, **24,** 273–309.

Sears, R. R., Maccoby, E. E., & Levin, H. *Patterns of child rearing.* Evanston, Ill.: Row, Peterson, 1957.

Sears, R. R., Pintler, M. H., & Sears, P. S. Effect of father separation on preschool children's doll play aggression. *Child development,* 1946, **17,** 219–243.

Shapiro, D., Crider, A. B., & Tursky, B. Differentiation of an automatic response through operant reinforcement. *Psychonomic Science,* 1964, **1,** 147–148.

Sherif, M., Harvey, O. J., White, B. J., Hood, W. R., & Sherif, C. W. *Intergroup conflict and cooperation. The Robbers' Cave experiment.* Norman, Okla.: University Book Exchange, 1961.

Sherif, M., & Sherif, C. W. *Reference groups.* New York: Harper & Row, 1964.

Sherif, M., & Sherif, C. W. Research on intergroup relations. In D. Klineberg and R. Christie. *Perspective in social psychology.* New York: Holt, Rinehart and Winston, 1965.

Shomer, R. W., Davis, A. H., & Kelley, H. H. Threats and the development of coordination: Further studies of the Deutsch and Krauss trucking game. *Journal of Personality and Social psychology,* 1966, **4,** 119–126.

Siegel, S. Individual decision making under risk. In H. Gulliksen and S. Messick, *Psychological scaling: Theory and applications.* New York: Wiley, 1960.

Siegel, S., & Fouraker, L. F. *Bargaining and group decision making.* New York: McGraw-Hill, 1960.

Simpson, G. E., & Yinger, J. M. *Racial and cultural-minorities.* New York: Harper & Bros., 1958.

Skinner, B. F. *Science and human behavior.* New York: Macmillan, 1953.

Skinner, B. F. *Verbal behavior.* New York: Appleton-Century-Crofts, 1957.

Skydell, R. Helping in children as a function of previously established habit of help-giving. Unpublished manuscript, Hunter College, 1967.

Solomon, R. L., & Wynne, L. C. Traumatic avoidance learning: The outcomes of several extinction procedures with dogs. *Journal of Abnormal and Social Psychology.* 1953, **48,** 291–302.

Spence, K. W. A theory of emotionally based drive (D) and its relation to performance in simple learning situations. *American Psychologist,* 1958, **13**, 131–141.

Stagner, R. Studies of aggressive social attitudes: I. measurement and interrelation of selected attitudes. *Journal of Social Psychology,* 1944, **20,** 10–20.

Stember, C. H. *Education and attitude change.* New York: Institute of Human Relations Press, 1961.

Stone, L. A. Social desirability and correlates of social responsibility. *Journal of Personality and Social Psychology,* 1965, **2,** 756–775.

Stone, L. A. Rejoinder to Berkowitz: Social desirability or social responsibility. *Journal of Personality and Social Psychology,* 1965, **2,** 758.

Stouffer, S. A., Suchman, E. A., DeVinney, L. C., Star, S. A., & Williams, R. M., Jr. *The American soldier. Adjustments during army life.* (Studies in psychology during World War II, Vol. 1). Princeton, N.J.: Princeton University Press, 1949.

Stratton, G. M. *Anger, its religious and moral significance.* New York: Macmillan, 1923.

Strodtbeck, F. I., James, R. M., & Hawkins, C. Social status in jury deliberations. In E. E. Maccoby, T. M. Newcomb, and E. L. Hartley, *Readings in social psychology.* New York: Holt, Rinehart and Winston, 1958.

Sullivan, P. L., & Adelson, J. Ethnocentrism and misanthrophy. *Journal of Abnormal* and *Social Psychology,* 1954, **49,** 246–249.

Sussman, M. The isolated nuclear family: Fact or fiction. *Social problems,* 1959, **6,** 333–340.

Tedeschi, R. E., Tedeschi, D. H., Mucha, A., Cook, L., Mattis, P. A., & Fellows E. J. Effects of various centrally acting drugs on fighting behavior of mice. *Journal of Pharmacological and Experimental Therapeutics,* 1959, **125,** 18.

Thibaut, J. W. An experimental study of the cohesiveness of underprivileged groups. *Human Relations,* 1950, **3,** 251–278.

Thibaut, J. W., & Coules, J. The role of communication in the reduction of interpersonal hostility. *Journal of Abnormal and Social Psychology,* 1952, **47,** 770–777.

Thibaut, J. W., & Kelley, H. H. *The social psychology of groups.* New York: Wiley, 1959.

Tinbergen, N. *The study of instinct.* London: Oxford University Press, 1951.

Tinbergen, N. *Social behavior in animals.* New York: Wiley, 1953.

Tolman, E. C. *Purposive behavior in animals and men.* New York: Century, 1932.

Tuchman, B. The guns of August. New York: Macmillan, 1962.

Ulrich, R. E., & Azrin, H. H. Reflexive fighting in reponse to aversive stimulation. *Journal of Experimental Analysis of Behavior,* 1962, **5,** 551–621.

Ulrich, R. E., Wolff, P. C., & Azrin, N. H. Shock as an elicitor of intra- and interspecies fiighting behavior. *Animal Behavior,* 1964, **12,** 145.

U.S. Supreme Court. *Brown v. Board of Education of Topeka* (1954) (347 U.S. 483).

Verplanck, W. S. The control of content of verbal behavior: Reinforcement of statement of opinion. *Journal of Abnormal and Social Psychology,* 1955, **51,** 668–676.

Walters, R. H., Leat, M., & Mezei, L. Response inhibition and disinhibition through empathetic learning. *Canadian Journal of Psychology,* 1963, **16,** 235–243.

Wasman, M., & Flynn, J. P. Directed attack elicited from the hypothalamus. *Archives of Neurology,* 1962, **6,** 220–227.

Watson, J. B., & Rayner, R. Conditioned emotional reactions. *Journal of Experimental Psychology,* 1920, **3,** 1–14.

Wertham, F. *Seduction of the innocent.* New York: Holt, Rinehart and Winston, 1954.

Wertham, F. *A sign for Cain.* New York: Macmillan, 1966.

Wheeler, L. Toward a theory of behavioral contagion. *Psychological Review,* 1966, **73,** 179–192.

Wheeler, L., & Levine, L. Observer-model similarity in the contagion of aggression. *Sociometry,* 1967, **30,** 41–49.

White, R. K. Images in the context of International conflicts: Soviet perceptions of the U.S. and U.S.S.R. In H. C. Kelman (Ed.), *International behavior.* New York: Holt, Rinehart and Winston, 1965.

White, R. K., & Lippitt, R. *Autocracy and democracy: And experimental inquiry.* New York: Harper, 1960.

Williams, R. M., Jr. The reduction of intergroup tensions. New York: Social Science Research Council Bulletin, 1947. pp. 57, 71.

Williams, R. M., Jr. *Strangers next door.* Englewood Cliffs, N.J.: Prentice-Hall, 1964.

Wrightsman, L. S. Personality and attitudinal correlates of trusting and trustworthy behaviors in a two-person game. *Journal of Personality and Social Psychology,* 1966, **4,** 328–333.

Wynne, L. C., & Solomon, R. L. Traumatic avoidance learning: Acquisition and extinction in dogs deprived of normal peripheral autonomic function. *Genetic Psychology Monographs,* 1955, **52,** 241–243.

Zener, L., & Kaufmann, H. Effects of reward structure and partner's cooperation upon strategy. Unpublished manuscript, University of Toronto, 1967.

Zimbardo, P. G., Cohen, A. R., Weisenberg, M., Dworkin, L., & Firestone, I. Control of pain motivation by cognitive dissonance. *Science,* 1966, **151,** 217–219.

NAME INDEX

SUBJECT INDEX

161

Social responsibility, 105–106
  scale, 111
Social scientist, 142
Social support, for aggression, 67, 68
Socialization, 120
  and cognitive processes, 51, 52
  and language, 51, 52
Socially responsible behavior, develop-
    ment, 128–134
  maintenance of, 128–134
Socially responsible values, 116
Stereotype, 80, 84, 90, 92, 138
Stimulus, 95, 135
  for aggression, 54, 136–137
  classification of, 122–123
  conditioned, 46, 103
  conditioned response to, 121
  social, 53
  unconditioned, 46, 103
  unconditioned for aggression, 61
Stimulus discrimination, 50
Stimulus generalization, 50
Superman, 21
Supreme Court, Brown Decision, 87
Symbolic mediation, 51, 52, 53, 121
Symbolic processes, 122

Tacitus, 92
Target, of aggression, 54, 55, 138
T.A.T., 6
Temperament, individual differences in,
    19
Thanatos, as destructive force, 14
Thucydides, 92
"True Believer," the, 93
Two-factor model of imitation, 49

Utility, 123, 125, 133, 142

Value, meaning of, 117, 118
Values, 53, 111, 133, 134, 142
  and behavior, 115–121
    noncorrespondence between, 98,
      102, 112–114, 116
  beneficial, 98–114
  and prejudice, 82
  transmission of, 56–57
Verbal behavior, 48–49
Victim, 136
  of aggression, 3, 54, 62–65
Visibility, and prejudice, 81

Words, in social learning, 48–59